The Natural History of Medicinal Plants

THE NATURAL HISTORY OF
MEDICINAL PLANTS

Judith Sumner

Foreword by Mark J. Plotkin

Timber Press
Portland, Oregon

Published in 2000 by
Timber Press, Inc.
The Haseltine Building
133 S.W. Second Avenue, Suite 450
Portland, Oregon 97204, U.S.A.

Library of Congress Cataloging-in-Publication Data
Sumner, Judith.
    The natural history of medicinal plants / Judith Sumner ; foreword by Mark
        Plotkin.
        p. cm.
    Includes bibliographical references and index.
    ISBN 0-88192-483-0
    1. Botany, Medical. 2. Medicinal plants. I. Title.
QK99.A1 S86 2000
581.6'34—dc21

                                                                    99-076555

Contents

Color plates follow page 144

Foreword

⁓

PLANTS have long served as our major source of medicinal compounds. The earliest writings from ancient Babylonia, Egypt, China, and India teem with references to healing herbs, indicating a prehistoric origin for the use of plants as medicines. With the advent of synthetic chemistry, however, much of the past century has seen a decreased reliance on botanicals as sources of original therapeutic compounds, particularly in the Western world. Most of the largest pharmaceutical companies had turned away from flowering plants in the (mistaken) belief that synthetic chemistry could cure the world's medical afflictions.

There is now an electrifying renaissance underway as these same firms realize that Mother Nature possesses answers to at least some of the medical questions we face. The computerization of the laboratory makes it possible to find, analyze, and manipulate molecules faster than ever before. Contrary to popular belief, these revolutionary technologies make the plant kingdom *more* important as a source of potential medicines. Given the appearance of "new" diseases like AIDS, as well as the frightening manifestations of drug-resistant strains of ancient killers like tuberculosis, the need for novel medications will continue to grow.

The skyrocketing interest in alternative and complementary ther-

9

apies also requires more and better information on medicinal plants. Current estimates suggest that between one-third and two-thirds of all Americans have experimented with nonallopathic medicine. Many of these therapies, such as herbalism, ayurvedic medicine, and aromatherapy, feature a botanical component. Yet most Western physicians are woefully uninformed when it comes to the subject of medicinal plants.

Judith Sumner's book could not appear at a better time. Interest in medicinal plants by the pharmaceutical industry and the general public is increasing, yet there is a dearth of recent, well-researched overviews on the past, present, and future of medicinal plants. This book fills that gap. It not only covers the historical uses of some of the most important species but also ventures into some of the most exciting research areas such as zoopharmacognosy, where scientists are learning of new and interesting compounds from plants used by animals! Because of its expansive scope, this book will be of use to everyone interested in gaining a broader understanding of the importance of medicinal plants. Whether you are an avid gardener, a practicing herbalist, or a physician whose patients want to know more about healing plants, this book belongs on your shelf.

MARK J. PLOTKIN, PH.D.
Amazon Conservation Team

Preface

$\sim$

THE IDEA for this book began with a medicinal botany course that I have taught for several years at the Arnold Arboretum of Harvard University and at the Garden in the Woods, the botanic garden of the New England Wild Flower Society in Framingham, Massachusetts. Lively student discussions and weekend field trips sparked the notion of a book that would consider the natural history of medicinal plants, the ecological significance of the botanical compounds used as medicines, and the history and present scope of medicinal botany.

With the passage of the 1994 Dietary Health and Education Act, interest in medicinal plants in the United States has grown rapidly, and the domestic market for medicinal herbs is rapidly approaching four billion dollars. Pushed heavily by the marketers of dietary supplements, and passed over the objections of the Food and Drug Administration, the act has been a source of great controversy. In brief, the act has allowed any substance that can be found naturally in foods to be sold in any quantity as a "dietary supplement" regardless of its natural concentrations or toxic potential. No premarket testing or Food and Drug Administration approval is necessary before selling such supplements, although the agency can certainly restrict sales if health problems later become known. In the case of the herb

Ephedra (ma huang), the Food and Drug Administration pulled it from the market after thirty-eight deaths were attributed to it.

While the passage of the 1994 act has been a boon to those who seek access to certain botanically derived medicines, it has also been the source of confusion. Although most supplements are purchased for medicinal properties, marketers are prohibited from making specific claims about health benefits, and consumers often base their purchasing decisions on inaccurate information passed along from a variety of sources, some more reliable than others. Standards for dose amounts, delivery systems, and overall quality do not exist, and *caveat emptor* is the watchword.

It is not the purpose of this book to insert itself into the food supplement and herbal medicines debate, but I do seek to provide in some way a balanced source of information that is accessible to the lay reader. Just as importantly, the purpose of this book is *not* to assist the reader in making decisions about which herbs to use or in which quantities. I do claim as my purpose to provide some scientific background for those interested in the natural history of medicinal plants. My goal has been to connect the human concerns of botanical medicines and ethnobotany with the role of medicinal plants and their secondary compounds in nature.

Acknowledgments

⌒

Laura Hastings of the Centre for Economic Botany and librarians at the Royal Botanic Gardens, Kew, located several historical documents. Barbara Pryor and the library staff at Garden in the Woods graciously lent research materials and photographs. Michael Huffman of the Primate Research Institute at Kyoto University supplied current information and photographs from his research with primates and medicinal plants; he also provided many useful insights about the new field of zoopharmacognosy. Paul Mahlberg of Indiana University kindly supplied a scanning electron micrograph of the surface trichomes of hemp. As a long-distance editor, Neal Maillet of Timber Press wrote thoughtful letters about style and content; he provided invaluable suggestions and certainly helped to turn a preliminary outline into a completed manuscript. Lastly, I am indebted to the many botany students who have motivated me through their interest and enthusiasm to see this project through to the end.

CHAPTER 1

~~~~~~

A Brief History of
Medicinal Botany

A VAST ARRAY of illnesses and medical complaints have always been and always will be a real part of the human condition. Plants have supplied humans with cures for their ailments, from relieving headaches to treating heart disease, since the time of earliest human evolution. The impact of plant-derived medicine on human history has been remarkable; opium, snakeroot, digitalis, feverbark, and chaulmoogra have all left their leaf prints on the human time line. These medicinal plants and others (both known and as yet undiscovered) are the foundation and the future of human medicine. The vast natural pharmacy of plant medicines once accounted for 80 percent of the substances used to cure disease, before we learned to synthesize medicinal compounds in the laboratory. Now about 40 percent of all medical prescriptions in the United States contain at least one plant-derived ingredient, and European physicians routinely recommend to their patients herbs such as chamomile and coneflower.

Plants in their natural habitats have "learned," in an evolutionary sense, to produce a fantastic storehouse of complex chemicals that we can exploit. We can use these medicines to curb and cure disease, a splendid coincidence for humankind. We will consider medicinal plants in their natural habitats and see that the production of complex chemicals has been a survival mechanism that has evolved as part of botanical biodiversity. Just as plant families can be distinguished by their flowers, leaves, and growth forms, in many cases plants can also be recognized by the chemicals that they produce as a defense against hungry animals.

Plant Medicines in Prehistory

The first good doctors were wise plant gatherers, early humans (but not necessarily "primitive") with a superior knowledge of practical botany. Which plants could be used reliably to cure infections, soothe croup, or halt tumorous growths? Plants can cause hallucinations, arousal or sedation, heart palpitations, fatal poisoning, or successful healing, depending upon the species and its chemical components. Prehistoric healers had knowledge of the specific practical chemistry of local plants and how to use them for effective cures.

Early knowledge of plant medicines was no doubt extensive and part of an oral tradition passed from healer to healer through generations in prehistory. Latin names, chemical formulas, and complex classifications had no place in the early arena of applied medicinal botany, yet the traditional knowledge of plant medicines was no doubt precise and acquired through careful observation and experimentation. Regrettably, we will never be able to credit the first healers who successfully paired curative plant medicines with human ailments, but their work was every bit as painstaking as the research that occurs today in pharmaceutical laboratories. We know from pollen evidence that medicinal plants were buried in Paleolithic graves, suggesting that knowledge of medicinal plants dates back at least sixty thousand years. That medicinal plants have been used for so long should come as no surprise, since ailments are as old as our species, and even nonhuman primates like chimpanzees and spider monkeys are known to consume plants with medicinal properties.

Early Records

The known written accounts of medicinal botany began about six thousand years ago. Some Sumerian clay tablets excavated from Nippur were cuneiform lists of botanical remedies. Despite their knowledge of mathematics and science, the Sumerians, Assyrians, and Babylonians attributed disease to supernatural agents, and they emphasized the role of priests and priestesses in divining cures. The practice of herbal medicine was left to specialists and scholars, such as the learned Assyrian King Ashurbanipal, who left behind tablets recording three hundred medicinal plants, including opium and myrrh.

The ancient Egyptians listed more than 850 plant medicines and remedies in the Ebers papyrus, a medical scroll seventy feet in length, sold to George Ebers by an Arab in the early 1870s. The scroll dates from about 1500 B.C. (Ebell translation, 1937). The Egyptian pharmacopoeia included such familiar medicinal plants as mandrake, aloe, castor bean, and opium. Garlic was believed to repel snakes and discourage tapeworms, and juniper berries from Lebanon were wrapped in mummies and used in purification ceremonies over corpses. Pyramid-building slaves were fed garlic and onions to prevent infections, while members of the royalty were entombed with a collection of herbal medicines, perfumes, and cosmetics to provide for their needs during their journey from mortality.

Among the earliest Sanskrit writings from about 1500 B.C., the *Rig Veda* is a poem that details medical information. These Hindu verses include mention of snakeroot (*Rauvolfia serpentina*), a plant that was used in India for thousands of years to treat snakebite and mental illness and for sedation. Despite its ancient uses, *Rauvolfia* first became known to Western medicine only about the middle of the twentieth century. Reserpine, its major active principle, depresses activity of the central nervous system, making it a valuable treatment for hypertension and schizophrenia. The *Rig Veda* provided the basis for the Ayurvedic system of medicine, which is still practiced in Hindu communities and includes more than fifteen hundred plant-derived medicines in its pharmacopoeia.

The Chinese emperor Shen Nung, who ruled about three thousand years ago, is credited with writing the first herbal, an illustrated book dealing with the gathering, preparation, and use of medicinal plants. The *Pen Tsao* described 365 medicinal plants that were used in ancient China, including several that are still used today: opium, ephedra, hemp, and chaulmoogra. Chaulmoogra, an oil derived from kalaw trees, was eventually "discovered" by Western physicians in the nineteenth century as the first successful cure for leprosy. Joseph Rock traveled to China in the early 1920s to collect kalaw seeds destined to be grown in Hawaiian plantations. Chaulmoogra oil is still used with sulfa drugs as an effective treatment against leprosy (now also known as Hansen's disease), a bacterial infection that has been a scourge for thousands of years.

Botanical Medicine in Early Europe

The Western tradition of medicine can be traced back to the Greek scholar and physician Hippocrates (460–377 B.C.), who believed that disease resulted from imbalance in the four bodily humors and advocated plant medicines to correct human ailments. Speaking of medical knowledge, Hippocrates recognized the overwhelming problem of learning by discovery a vast body of medical information: "Life is short and the art [of medicine] is long, the occasion fleeting, experience fallacious and judgment difficult." (All translations of Hippocrates come from *Nature's Pharmacy: A History of Plants and Healing* by Christine Stockwell, 1988.) Modern pharmaceutical researchers would no doubt agree.

Hippocrates' approach was purely rational, and he rejected diagnoses and cures that were based on magic. He rejected the prevalent idea that epileptic fits came from consuming goat meat or using goat skins, as well as a competing theory that epilepsy was a sacred ailment. He observed that a connection exists between outlook and illness, stating bluntly: "Our natures are the physicians of our diseases." Nevertheless, he relied upon three hundred plant species to heal his patients; these were primarily purgatives and emetics, prescribed with the object of correcting internal imbalances by ejecting the offending humors from the patient. He left us the Hippocratic oath, which reflects awareness of the dangers of plant medicines if they are used carelessly: "I will give no deadly drug to any, though it be asked of me, nor will I counsel such."

Theophrastus (371–287 B.C.), a student of Plato and Aristotle, wrote extensively on plant subjects and is considered the first real botanist. He rejected the mysterious practices that were associated with collecting certain important medicinal plants. Frightening legends were spread during his time about the dangers of collecting plants such as mandrake and peony; Theophrastus realized that collectors need not fear attack by woodpeckers while gathering peonies, nor did collectors need to pray while collecting hellebore. His work *Historia Plantarum* covered the collection and preparation of plant medicines, spices, and perfumes and was used for two thousand years as a reliable reference.

With the rise of Rome, many Greek physicians immigrated to parts of the Roman empire where medicine was accomplished practically by herb gatherers and peddlers, slaves, and older women who were knowledgeable in applied botany. Much of Hippocrates' practical teaching was forgotten, but when Julius Caesar elevated Greek physicians to Roman citizenship in 46 B.C., plant medicines soon enjoyed some higher regard.

As a young man, Pedanios Dioscorides (first century A.D.) assembled *De Materia Medica*, a comprehensive treatment of the properties, uses, cultivation, and selection of six hundred medicinal plants. He traveled as a surgeon with Nero's army, which broadened his experience as a field botanist with comprehensive knowledge of European medicinal plants. Dioscorides recognized botanical subtleties. He knew that time of day and flowering time can influence potency of medicines, for instance, opium. We now know that an opium poppy capsule contains four times more morphine if the latex is collected in the early morning. Dioscorides advocated the use of a decoction of white willow for painful gout, a practice used traditionally as an external remedy for pain for the next several centuries. This use foreshadowed the development of aspirin in 1899 by the Bayer Company of Germany. Aspirin (acetylsalicylic acid) comes from the willow-derived compound salicin.

De Materia Medica resembled a modern pharmacopoeia in many ways because Dioscorides included not only descriptions and illustrations of medicinal plants but also information about their preparation, use, and side effects. Since the ancient Greeks left the practical work of obtaining medicinal plants to root diggers, or *rhizotomi,* a caste of expert plant collectors who specialized in medicinal species, a standard well-illustrated reference was invaluable to physicians, *rhizotomi,* and patients alike. *De Materia Medica* was used as a resource for the next fifteen centuries; it was the standard reference through the Middle Ages, a time when physicians acquired little additional knowledge of medicinal plants.

Despite such strong reliance on the writings of Greek physicians, some facts of ancient Greek medicine were misplaced for centuries. Recent evidence suggests that Greeks and Romans relied upon plants for population control. Both Queen Anne's lace (*Daucus carota*) and silphium (now extinct, but most likely a species of *Ferula,* a large rel-

Figure 1-1. Queen Anne's lace (*Daucus carota*) was used by Greek and Roman women for abortion and contraception.

ative of cultivated fennel) were ingested by women of childbearing age, apparently to limit births. Hippocrates advised the use of Queen Anne's lace for contraception and abortion, and the Roman poet Catullus (ca. 84–54 B.C.) made a veiled reference to silphium in a romantic poem to a lover. In rodents the seeds of Queen Anne's lace can block the synthesis of progesterone, a hormone necessary for the successful completion of a pregnancy. Silphium was extinct by the third or fourth century A.D., probably due to overcollection, but a related member of the genus *Ferula* is now used as an abortifacient by practitioners of folk medicine in central Asia. The active ingredient in silphium, ferujol, is nearly 100 percent effective in preventing pregnancies in laboratory rats and may well have provided similar benefits in ancient times for women who sought to limit the number of children that they bore. Other plants, such as pennyroyal (*Hedeoma pulegioides*), a mint, and seeds of the edible pomegranate (*Punica granatum*), may also have provided some additional early sources of oral contraceptives. In subsequent chapters, we will consider the benefits from a plant's perspective of being able to produce chemicals that can disrupt the reproduction of herbivores.

The Medieval Period

In the early days of European Christianity, the practice of medicine abandoned rational science and turned to church dogma for medical explanations and methods. At the end of the fourth century, Christians burned the temple of Zeus at Alexandria in northern Egypt, which housed a medical school and a library of seven hundred thousand books, including many medical texts. Practical medicine was done by barber-surgeons and monks, who were as likely to prescribe purging and repentance as the botanical medicines familiar to ancient peoples. A ninth-century poem, *De Cultura Hortorum,* described the medicinal plants growing in a monastery garden.

Monastery libraries preserved classical writings in botany and medicine until they would be read again. Simultaneously, the Chinese were updating Shen Nung's herbal, and the Arabs were building a new hospital at Baghdad and translating Greek and Roman texts. Avicenna (980–1037) became court physician in Persia by age eighteen, and his *Canon of Medicine* was used for the next five hundred years. His likeness has appeared on the diploma of the Pharmaceutical Society of Great Britain since the founders received their charter from Queen Victoria. Arabs also had a hand in founding the great medical school in Salerno, Italy, where scholars wrote the *Antidotarium Nicolai,* an early European text on drugs. Reliance on plant medicines remained intense. Michael Scott (ca. 1175–1230), a retainer and "wondrous wizard" in the court of Frederick II of Germany, began as a medical student at Salerno. He developed a reliable anesthetic for surgery that could be inhaled from a cloth; this potentially

Figure 1-2. Followers of the Doctrine of Signatures imagined a human body in the branched roots of mandrake (*Mandragora officinarum*), which suggested its use as a panacea to treat a variety of human ills.

lethal botanical mixture contained henbane, opium, and mandrake.

Medievals relied on the Doctrine of Signatures to help them know and recognize medicinal plants. It was the Chinese who first conceived that the medical use of a plant could be detected through "signatures," clues revealed by shape, taste, texture, and color. If a plant resembled a particular body part such as the liver or heart, its physical form was regarded as a suggestion for its use. Many early vernacular names such as heartsease, boneset, eyebright, toothwort, liverwort, and maidenhair reveal the uses of medicinal plants that were suggested by the Doctrine of Signatures. Eyebrights are various daisies with brightly colored centers, which suggested their use for clearing the eyes and improving vision. Boneset has pairs of leaves fused across the stem, which hinted at its use for healing broken bones, while the black, shiny stalks of maidenhair fern (Plate 2) recommended it for healthy hair. Perhaps the most valued of the signatures appeared in mandrake; the branched roots may vaguely resemble a human form, which recommended them as a panacea to treat all human ills. The notion of signatures, however far-fetched, was probably appealing because it proposed to make some sense of the enormous task of relating ailment with treatment. The Doctrine of Signatures spread throughout Europe during the Middle Ages as part of the oral tradition.

An epidemic of plague (or black death), a severe bacterial infection caused by *Yersinia pestis,* worked its way through Europe during the fourteenth century. At least half the population succumbed; the sick and dying were tended to by brave physicians, who ventured out in the streets wearing leather hoods and face cones filled with aromatic herbs. Tremendous faith was placed in plants with aromatic pungency. Bouquets of pungent species such as wormwood (*Artemisia*) were also used in law courts to combat infections that might be carried by prisoners.

Herbals and Herbalists of the Renaissance

There were no known effective medicines to combat plague, but a Renaissance herbalist nevertheless acquired his reputation as a knowledgeable physician during a 1529 epidemic of "English sweating sickness" in Germany. Leonhard Fuchs (1501–1566) authored the scholarly herbal *De Historia Stirpium* (1542), in which he compiled the medicinal uses of five hundred plant species, four hundred of them native to Germany. He worked with two artists and a draftsman to render remarkably accurate botanical woodcuts to illustrate his Latin text, which was soon translated into German as the *New Kreuterbuch*. The illustrations were drawn from real specimens, and at the end of *De Historia Stirpium* the illustrators are themselves shown hard at work with their plants and tools. The herbal included the first European illustrations of some New World species such as corn and pumpkins. Fuchs's accurate woodcuts were reprinted and copied as illustrations in several other herbals produced during the next century, including Bock's *Kreuter Buch* in Germany and Turner's *New Herball* in England. His text consists of an alphabetical listing and description of medicinal plants, much of it derived from Dioscorides. Nevertheless, Fuchs's pleasure in working as field botanist shines through in his comment: "[T]here is nothing in this life that is pleasanter and more delightful than to wander over woods, mountains, plains, garlanded and adorned with flowerlets of various sorts, and to gaze intently upon them."

Another outstanding herbalist was Otto Brunfels (1464–1534), who turned from a monastic career to teaching and eventually to medicine, becoming the town physician of Bern. His three-volume herbal *Herbarum Vivae Eicones* (1530–1536) pioneered the practice of drawing specimens from life, rather than slavishly copying earlier illustrations with little regard for the actual appearance of the plant. His artist, Hans Weiditz, has received little recognition, but his contributions were considerable. He insisted on illustrating plants that were unknown to ancient botanists and physicians; Brunfels considered such plants to be outcast "herbae nudae" because they lacked names from antiquity, but he was forced by Weiditz to include their "portraits" in his herbal. The result was a complete work that included many more medicinal species that Brunfels otherwise would have overlooked.

Weiditz drew from life, and his accurate illustrations of medicinal plants include natural imperfections like damaged leaves and with-

Figure 1-3. An illustration of hellebore (*Helleborus viridis*) from *Herbarum Vivae Eicones,* vol. 1 (1530), reveals the natural detail of a species valued since ancient times as a medicine and a poison.

ered flowers. In the text Brunfels held tenaciously to his revered "ancient and trustworthy authors," although his worthy goal was to revive the study of plants, to "bring back life to a science almost extinct." As the title of the herbal suggests, it did provide "living portraits of plants," but Brunfels's downfall was a complete disregard for plant geography. Theophrastus had noted almost eighteen hundred years earlier that each region of the earth had its characteristic flora, yet Brunfels was determined to find the same plants near Strasbourg that Dioscorides had enumerated in the Mediterranean region. In the end, the text of *Herbarum Vivae Eicones* was fraught with discrepancies.

Hieronymus Bock (1498–1554), a contemporary of Brunfels, also spent time in a monastery and as a teacher, eventually turning to the Lutheran ministry and medicine to make a living. His *New Kreuterbuch* (1539) originally lacked illustrations, but he compensated for this with clear paragraphs describing the life histories of herbaceous plants he observed in the field firsthand, from the time of their first appearance to the end of the growing season. Bock tested superstitions, rather than repeating them verbatim from other authors, but somehow he imagined that he observed ferns (*Osmunda* spp., which all reproduce by spores) produce seeds at midnight on Saint John's eve. Six years later, an illustrated edition of the herbal appeared (renamed *Kreuter Buch*), with many illustrations borrowed from Fuchs and other sources. Some original woodcuts of useful plants were made by David Kandel of Strasbourg, an artist who broke with form and included people and animals in his botanical illustrations.

Bock's herbal sold more copies than those of Brunfels and Fuchs, but all three books were issued in various editions, including smaller "field guide" herbals for use in the countryside or garden. The text was sometimes omitted altogether, and the woodblocks and prose were copied and recopied endlessly. The original folio edition of Fuchs's *De Historia Stirpium* weighed more than eleven pounds; a miniature edition published by Jean de Tournes in 1555 could fit easily in a pocket.

These books were not the only available herbals. The invention of the printing press in mid-fifteenth-century Europe allowed book production more easily than ever before. There were many other herbalists throughout Europe during the fifteenth, sixteenth, and seventeenth centuries writing and illustrating books of medicinal plants. Local print shops also produced quantities of anonymous herbals for the general trade, illustrated with crude woodcuts and often with such generic titles as *Gart der Gesundheit* (garden of health) and *Hortus Sanitatus* (plants of health). These herbals were among the first "mass-marketed" books. As an addition to the available herbals, botanist Valerius Cordus (1515–1544) compiled a list of useful directions for preparing plant medicines for consumption, which he presented in manuscript form to the physicians of Nuremberg. Eventually it was published by the town council about 1546 as the *Dispensatorium*. This publication was the first pharmacopoeia, an official listing of medicines along with information on their preparation and use.

The herbalists of England also compiled some noteworthy works. Richard Bancke's *Herbal* (1525) recommended using rosemary against "venymous serpentes," "evyll dremes," and melancholy; the popularity of his herbal was revealed by its frequent reprinting under various titles. Peter Treveris cautioned his readers in *The Grete Herball* (1526) against drug "fraude" and the dangers of water for drinking and bathing. Melancholy could be reversed with artemesia and aristolochia, while a cough called for licorice, and scalds required olive oil. Reason prevailed in William Turner's *New Herball* (1551–1562), in which superstition, mythology, and the Doctrine of Signatures were aggressively refuted. As a physician educated at Pembroke College of Cambridge, he rejected the Doctrine of Signatures's notion of mandrake significance because its branched taproot may (with imagination) resemble a human torso. He alleged that humanoid mandrake roots are "conterfited . . . folishe feined trifles, and not naturall."

John Gerard (1545–1612) was a successful gardener who compiled the best-known English herbal, *The Herball or Generall Historie of Plantes* (1597). Neither the text nor the illustrations are original; Gerard relied on an incomplete translation of an earlier Belgian herbal by Dodoens, completed the translation, rearranged text, and added illustrations acquired from the German herbalist Jakob Theodor. His scientific sense was nil, illustrated by his sincere account of the legend of a shell-bearing tree that hatches barnacle geese. Gerard recommended stamping bruises with the cut root of Solomon's seal, good for "women's willfillnesse in stumbling upon their hasty husbands' fists." Thomas Johnson, a London apothecary, published a revised edition of *The Herball* in 1633. With Johnson as editor, the errors were corrected, new woodcuts added, and 2850 medicinal plants were described.

The last of the English herbalists also came from the gardening tradition. John Parkinson (1567–1650), who became apothecary to King James I, was a botanist with a well-known London garden. His early work *Paradisi in Sole Paradisi Terrestris* (1629) is a gardening text, rather than an herbal. (The title includes an amusing Latin pun on his name; "paradisi in sole" translates literally as park-in-sun.) His later mammoth volume, *Theatrum Botanicum: The Theatre of Plants. Or, an Herball of a Large Extent* (1640), borrowed botanical information from earlier Dutch and Swiss manuscripts, and several illustrations were copied from Gerard. Parkinson did not entirely reject folk mythology, however, as revealed by his discussion of unicorn horn and powdered mummy as cures for human ills.

The Doctrine of Signatures was still embraced with enthusiasm by many scholars, such as the astronomer Giambattista della Porta (1535–1605). His *Phytognomonica* (1588) provided detailed illustrations of plants with heart-shaped leaves, fruits, and bulbs as recommended cures for heart ailments. Pine cones, thistles, catkins, and lily bulbs and other scaly plant parts were proposed as solutions for skin diseases. He mixed logic and science liberally with magic and superstition in an attempt to work out a simple method of prescribing plant medicines for human ills. In doing so, he was the first

Figure 1-4. The decorative frontispiece from the 1633 edition of John Gerard's *The Herball* illustrates some of the New World plants such as "Turkie Wheate" or corn (*Zea mays*) that are included in the volume.

to describe the Doctrine of Signatures formally. Some of his notions were far-fetched even for the time; long-lived plants would lengthen a person's life, and moss gathered from a human skull would be useful in curing diseases of the head. Parkinson went so far as to illustrate *muscus ex craneo humano* in *Theatrum Botanicum*. The correlations proposed by Della Porta were often obscure, with pomegranate seeds suggested for strong teeth, plants with jointed stems recommended for scorpion stings, and walnuts advised for brain complaints. If plant signatures were not enough, his belief in natural astrology provided even more material for medical theorizing.

Another name associated with the Doctrine of Signatures is Theophrastus Bombastus von Hohenheim (1493–1551), Paracelsus by self-proclamation, a mystic and physician. He confidently rejected ancient teachings, despite his meager knowledge of botany. Paracelsus

Figure 1-5. Plants recommended for treating skin diseases in *Phytognomonica* (1588) included structures with sloughing layers like onion bulbs or scaly surfaces such as thistles and pine cones.

observed that the leaves of St. John's wort bear small impressed dots and its crushed flowers yield a red juice, which to him signified its use for treating wounds. St. John's wort is now being investigated as a possible source of medicinal compounds to combat psychological depression.

During the Renaissance in Europe, an herbal was also being written in the New World. After being compiled by Martin de la Cruz, an Aztec physician, and Juannes Badianus, an Aztec lecturer at the Roman Catholic College of Santa Cruz, the Badianus herbal was brought to Italy and ultimately deposited in the Vatican library. Eventually the manuscript was rediscovered in 1931, and a second, more crude copy from 1600 has also been found. Some of the 180 New World species such as mimosa and sedum are easily recognized, but the identification of several other plants remains a mystery. Although Badianus translated the manuscript into Latin, the stylized illustrations are identified by their Aztec names. One pink-flowered herb is drawn with ants on its roots, identified only as "medicine from an ant hill." As with many European herbals, the Badianus illustrations are drawn to reveal the nature of the underground parts such as roots, rhizomes, and bulbs. These subterranean structures are often the most potent part of a medicinal plant, where the secondary compounds produced by metabolism are most concentrated.

What's in a Name?

The confusion over plant names and identities in the Badianus herbal foreshadows what would become a growing problem in botany and botanical medicine: the need for a universal, efficient system of plant naming. Through the first half of the eighteenth century, botanists and physicians alike relied on Latin names, each a short descriptive phrase, for identification. The number of known plants was increasing daily as world exploration burgeoned. Latin phrase names (so-called polynomials) became longer and more descriptive to account for the variation in related groups of plants.

Thus the name for belladonna, a medicinal plant whose properties were recognized by medievals, was *atropa caule herbaceo, foliis ovatus integris*. The phrase translates roughly as "the atropa with herbaceous stems and entire, oval leaves," too cumbersome and lengthy for routine use.

In 1753 the Swedish botanist Carl Linnaeus broke with tradition in developing his system of binomial nomenclature, which he first used consistently in his two-volume work *Species Plantarum* (kinds of plants). As an experienced botanist and physician (*Species Plantarum* was published just a few weeks before his forty-sixth birthday), Linnaeus knew thousands of plants firsthand, probably more than any other person of his time, and he toiled with their classification. No doubt, he had become exasperated with polynomials.

Linnaeus developed binomial nomenclature more or less accidentally, originally as a convenient shorthand method for a listing of plants and animals that he found on two Baltic islands during a state-sponsored exploration in 1741. By 1753, he had the system perfected and was prepared to try it out on all the plant species that he knew. The Latin polynomials (along with references to the work of earlier botanists) still appear in *Species Plantarum,* but a one-word descriptive epithet is also listed in the margin next to the entry for each species. A species is known by the name of its genus followed by the epithet for that species; thus belladonna efficiently becomes *Atropa belladonna*. Many ancient Greek names such as *Daucus* (Queen Anne's lace), *Crataegus* (hawthorn), and *Asparagus* were still in use, and Linnaeus preserved these as the names of genera.

In his effort to classify all known plants, Linnaeus included many medicinal plants in *Species Plantarum* such as mandrake, feverbark, and digitalis. No particular mention is made of their medicinal uses, possibly because just a few years before he had published *Materia Medica* (1749), a reference book for physicians. This invaluable work included information on illnesses and specific medicines, pharmaceutical effects, dosage, and country of origin of the medicinal plants. Ever the classifier, Linnaeus provided information on medicinal plant names and their synonyms to alleviate some ongoing confusion over names. Medicinal plants and food plants invited turmoil because their names and identities were often subject to scrutiny.

With the acceptance of binomial nomenclature by botanists, Linnaeus gave us a system of naming that has survived nearly 250 years. *Species Plantarum* is now considered the starting point for plant names, including the names of medicinal plants. In determining the correct scientific name of a plant, botanists ignore all names predating 1753, even names of medicinal plants that appear in ancient writings and herbals. The legacy of these early botanists and physicians persists in many common names and the ancient names that were preserved by Linnaeus in *Species Plantarum*. As a final note of interest, twinflower (*Linnaea borealis*), a woodland wildflower that Linnaeus named for himself, had several New World medicinal uses that were probably unknown to Linnaeus. The Algonquin Indians prepared an infusion of the entire plant to drink during pregnancy, and the Iroquois treated childhood fevers and cramps with a decoction of the stems. As a plant with a northern circumpolar distribution, twinflower is known from Greenland, Labrador, Alaska, Newfoundland, Nova Scotia, and the United States. It does not appear in European herbals but was well known to Native Americans as part of their local medicinal flora.

The Nineteenth Century

The connection between botany and medicine persisted well into the nineteenth century. Charles Darwin (1809–1882) studied medicine at Edinburgh and later, as a naturalist, made extensive botanical studies on plant movement, distribution, pollination, and breeding. He corresponded with the American botanist Asa Gray (1810–1888), who also had trained as a physician but abandoned medicine to study plants. Gray depended on plants to cure his patients; in a letter to a colleague he mentioned a mixture of "ground Mustard and black pepper, mixed up with vinegar" for croup and bronchitis. His professional interests, however, lay in the natural world rather than the sickroom. He wrote the *Manual of the Botany of the Northern United States* (1848), the major reference for plant identification in eastern North America.

By the mid-nineteenth century, few medical doctors in the United States maintained their physic gardens or foraged in the woods for their patients' prescriptions, but they knew where to find the most pure, fresh, and clearly labeled medicinal plants. Their source was often the thriving wholesale medicinal herb business begun by the Shakers, a small religious order that had arrived in America from England in the 1770s. By 1826 there were eighteen Shaker communities in the United States, and several participated in the business of gathering, growing, processing, and packaging more than four hundred medicinal plants that were sold exclusively to physicians and pharmacists. The comprehensive catalogs of the Shakers advertised native American and European plants, listed by common and botanical names, and accuracy was the rule. The Shaker herb business followed strict policies that helped to produce a consistent product. When plants were harvested, only one type was gathered at a time to avoid confusion; herbs were collected when they were ripe and dry, bark was stripped from trees in the spring, and dug roots were cleaned of all debris and soil.

Shaker medicinal plants were well advertised and sold to members of the medical profession during a time in which questionable herbal cures were aggressively marketed to a believing public. Several species that were cultivated in Shaker communities are notoriously toxic, including black henbane (*Hyoscyamus niger*) and Jimson weed or thorn apple (*Datura stramonium*), herbs that could only be safely administered by a physician. Such potentially deadly plants, whether European or native in origin, could not be sipped in herbal teas with impunity. The catalogs invited "medical men" to sample a variety of medicinal herbs listed with specific claims for their curative powers; mayflower or gravel plant (*Epigaea repens;* Plate 17) was advertised for kidney stones ("gravel"), and butterfly weed or pleurisy root (*Ascle-*

pias tuberosa; Plate 8) could be "Combined with a tea of Skunk Cabbage" for relief of chest inflammations.

The Shakers prepared and sold their herbal mixtures such as liverwort syrup and pills for digestion made of "extracts of our indigenous plants." These products were a sign of the times. Patent medicines, many with bogus claims, flooded the marketplace in the mid-nineteenth century; these included herbal extracts and elixirs that were promoted with dubious testimonials of their efficacy. In 1849, the House of Representatives made a report to the Thirtieth Congress criticizing patent drugs as "an evil over which the friends of science and humanity never cease to mourn," but the Shakers' superior botanical knowledge kept them out of the fray and encouraged professional confidence in their products.

The Shaker community of Harvard, Massachusetts, began its herb business by gathering local plants to prepare as medicines for home use. On extended forays they gathered native New England plants from their wild habitats in forests and swamps, and by the 1820s they cultivated medicinal plants and operated an herb house for drying and processing. By the 1850s their catalogs listed 212 herbs for sale. The Harvard Shakers were sufficiently confident in their products to ship a set of prepared extracts and herb cakes to the Royal Botanic Gardens, Kew, where British botanists acknowledged the gift with a parchment scroll and added the collection to their museum of economic botany. Ironically, these Shakers were not among the several Shaker communities that cultivated the native American bee balm or Oswego tea (*Monarda didyma;* Plate 21) that replaced tea after the Boston Tea Party in 1773. Shakers advertised Oswego tea for stomach upsets; we now know that its component thymol is antiseptic and that the tea provides a mild sedative effect.

Shakers relied on European introductions and native American plants to supply their herb business, obtaining seed and introducing new plants into cultivation as necessary. As with the first medicinal gardens in New England, plants escaped from Shaker gardens and became naturalized and integrated into the local flora. Culver's root

(*Veronicastrum virginicum*) is rare in New England, but a field of the tall plants flowers each summer on land that was owned and cultivated by the Harvard Shaker community. Seneca Indians used Culver's root as a purgative, and the Shakers sold the dried root as a laxative; the fresh root is too effective to be used safely. Purple angelica (*Angelica atropurpurea*), once advertised by the Shakers for colic and stomach pain, today thrives in an adjacent wet meadow on land also once owned by the Shaker community. As a tangible link to the past, both species also exist as dried specimens in the herbarium made more than 140 years ago by Elisha Myrick, the industrious Harvard Shaker who ran the community's lucrative herb business for decades.

Medicinal Chemistry

A new field of study, organic chemistry, was on the scientific horizon at the beginning of the nineteenth century. Scientists believed that complex chemicals occurring in organisms, such as the compounds that are the "active ingredients" in medicinal plants, could only be made in living tissues. The idea was that there was a "vital force" behind the synthesis of these so-called organic compounds, which made them impossible to produce in the laboratory. Eventually this notion was disproven by the German chemist Friedrich Wöhler, who in 1828 accidentally made urea (an animal waste product) in the laboratory. Over the next two decades, more organic compounds were synthesized by chemists, and the "vital force" concept was laid to rest along with phlogiston theory and other disproven scientific notions.

Organic chemistry is now known as the chemistry of carbon compounds, particularly those in which a chain of carbon atoms forms the backbone of the molecule. Tars from coal and wood were used as the starting points for synthesis of new medicines. Plants were no longer among the few sources for effective medicines; organic compounds could be synthesized by chemists in the laboratory. The first edition of the *United States Pharmacopoeia* (1820) listed

650 drugs, of which 70 percent, or 455, were from plants. The eleventh edition of the *USP* (1936) listed 570 drugs, but the percentage of plant-derived medicines had dropped to only 40 percent (260) of the total. Between 1920 and 1936, many plant-derived compounds were no longer recognized by the federal government as effective medicines; they were being replaced by synthetic organic compounds.

The trend toward synthetic medicines was reversed in part in the years before World War II, when Western medicine discovered antibiotics such as penicillin and actinomycin. With renewed interest in medicines from natural products, additional plant-derived drugs have appeared in the pharmaceutical marketplace: muscle relaxants from curare, blood anticoagulants from sweet clover, anticancer alkaloids from Madagascar periwinkles, tranquilizers from *Rauvolfia* species, and oral contraceptives derived from molecular precursors in tropical yams. Some plant compounds still must come directly from plants because they have not yet been successfully synthesized, including morphine, cocaine, ergotamine, podophyllin, and digitalis. Other plant compounds such as atropine and reserpine are too expensive to synthesize, so pharmaceutical companies continue to rely on natural sources.

Future Directions

Medicinal botany is still a vastly unknown field. Systematic botanists estimate that there are at least 250,000 species of flowering plants and that fewer than 5 percent have been investigated for their medicinal potential, despite years of human interaction with plants as our primary source of effective medicines. The greatest number of unknown species is around the equator and consists of tropical forest plants that are threatened with extinction as their habitats are destroyed. The situation demands attention, but tropical diversity is too extensive to rely exclusively on random screening to locate potential new drugs.

Much current interest in medicinal botany focuses on the relatively new field of ethnobotany, the study of plant uses by indigenous peoples. The oral tradition of cultures that were once considered "primitive" will now suggest the most fruitful areas of research for the public and private pharmaceutical laboratories of developed nations. Other poorly understood areas of medicine, such as the traditional medicine practiced in China, will provide starting points for significant research into new effective drugs. With access to knowledge from diverse cultures, we will continue to grapple with the fundamental problem: Illness is part of the human condition, and plants provide potential cures. Like our forebears, we must continue to work deliberately to discover the connections between disease and cure; the history of medicinal botany is still in its beginning stages.

CHAPTER 2

～

Acquiring Knowledge

A CHILD lies gravely ill; relatives gather at the bedside while doctors confer nearby. Whether in a teaching hospital or rain forest hut, this scene reflects fear and hope, our vulnerability to disease, and the need for cures in time of serious illness. Specialized knowledge of medicines, whether the Food and Drug Administration–approved vincristine for childhood leukemia or a shaman's mixture for fever, takes generations to acquire. The basic research leading to the discovery of new plant medicines may be accomplished equally well in a pharmaceutical laboratory or in a shaman's home. Here we will explore the acquisition of such knowledge: How did people first learn about plant medicines? How do we continue to investigate medicinal plants and learn to apply their compounds to human illnesses? Which plants remain to be studied and understood for their medicinal potential?

Our ancestors were curious explorers of the natural world, perhaps most actively in times of deprivation or food scarcity. Plants were tasted and categorized as edible, toxic, hallucinogenic, unpalatable, unpleasant, or medicinal. Medicinal species were probably used on a trial-and-error basis, the early beginnings of the arduous, ongoing project of correlating drug plants with diseases and conditions that they relieve or cure. A practical understanding of dose was no doubt part of early learning, since many medicinal species are also extremely toxic.

Early humans attributed disease and death to supernatural forces but relied on the chemistry of plant compounds to provide cures. Treatment began with the pathway to finding a cure, possibly through divination, which had its roots in prehistory and early magic. Some rain forest healers still interact with a spirit world using hallucinogenic plants to induce the mental state necessary to communicate with supernatural forces. To practitioners of Western medicine, such customs are remarkably unscientific, but some aspects of modern medicine can also border on the interface between science and religion. The expert local healers, shamans, or medicine men know such hallucinogenic plants as the Andean genus *Brugmansia* and the related genera *Methysticodendron* and *Brunfelsia*. Practitioners in effect "own," cultivate, and propagate selected forms of *Brugmansia* such as *B. suaveolens* that have been found in nature; some of these medicinal plants may represent virally infected forms of species that occur in nature. The leaves of the less potent varieties are macerated in water, which releases their abundant psychoactive tropane alkaloids, and this infusion is used to induce divination.

Methysticodendron is known only from plants cultivated by Indian medicine men in the Valley of Sibundoy, Colombia. The plants are probably virally infected species of *Brugmansia,* now so atrophied in their growth that positive identification is impossible. Besides divination, *Methysticodendron* is used as a plaster or bath to treat tumors, fevers, chills, and swollen joints. The plants contain tropane alkaloids such as scopolamine and atropine, which need not be consumed orally to induce their effects. Tropane alkaloids are fat-soluble and can pass quickly through skin layers. Scopolamine induces intoxication and hallucination, followed by unconsciousness; atropine ingestion results in blurred vision and vasodilation, along with agitation and delirium.

In divination, the healer essentially swallows the medicine as part of realizing a cure for the patient, and more than one plant may be used to induce the required mental state. The Tarahumara Indians of northern Mexico use a species of *Tillandsia,* a pineapple relative, to augment the hallucinogenic effects of the peyote cactus (*Lophophora williamsii*) during healing rituals. Later the patient may also be dosed with another plant-derived medicine, presumably once guidance is received from supernatural forces. The Tarahumara use Jimson weed (*Datura stramonium*), a close relative of *Brugmansia* (sometimes interpreted taxonomically as the same genus), as a potent all-purpose drug. They believe that Jimson weed originated in the hellish lower

Figure 2-1. *Brugmansia suaveolens* produces tropane alkaloids, psychoactive compounds used by local Andean healers to induce the altered mental state associated with divination.

part of the universe and that unqualified collectors run the risk of insanity and death if they gather the potent plant. Both genera have concentrated amounts of scopolamine, which may also have been used as a hallucinogenic component of externally applied witches' brews in Roman and Medieval Europe.

Magic aside, how might divination lead to greater knowledge of plant medicines and their applications? As an ancient practice, divination may represent a way to induce deep concentration and introspective thought, in which a local healer formulates a treatment plan based on his encyclopedic knowledge of local botany and practical medicine.

All knowledge of medicinal plants depends on experimentation; somebody had to swallow the first mouthful of macerated roots or sip the first leaf infusion to assess the possible medicinal effects of a new plant. In the living laboratory of the forest, variables abound. Certain populations of a plant species may be more potent than others, and plant parts vary in their concentrations of medicinal compounds. Roots often have high concentrations of secondary compounds, which explains why root structure was carefully illustrated in early herbals and why Greek gatherers of medicinal species were known as root diggers. Chemical content can also vary with the maturity of the plant and the season of the year. In the Asian opium poppy (*Papaver somniferum*) the alkaloid mixture known as opium is present in the wall of the maturing capsule for only eight to ten days in the plant's life cycle. The first knowledge of the soporific and analgesic properties of opium most likely depended on the serendipitous collection of the chemically laden latex at just that critical time. We can envision the trial and error that led to an understanding of how and when to harvest opium, its addictive properties, and its potential to alleviate human suffering. Despite the addictive qualities of morphine, which is just one of the twenty-six opium alkaloids, opium has provided relief for everything from teething discomfort to the pain associated with battlefield wounds and terminal cancer. Knowledge of the opium poppy also led to the development of heroin, a semi-synthetic derivative of morphine and acetic acid; originally heroin was considered a nonaddictive form of morphine, but quite the converse is true. The nineteenth-century opium wars in China were the result of widespread opium addiction, which affected about a quarter of the Chinese population. The potential for addiction is an unfortunate side effect of some alkaloids, including morphine and cocaine, in which case self-medication with a medicinal plant or its purified compounds becomes an illness in itself.

Poison or Medicine, Toxin or Drug?

With most medicinal plants the amount used in therapy is critical, since many medicinal compounds are often toxins as well. Innocuous herbs such as the various mints can be used with impunity in teas and infusions, but in other cases the determination of dose is challenging and dangerous work. Since prehistory, deaths have occurred as the result of poisoning with plant medicines that were introduced as therapies. Then, as now, unintentional mistakes did occur. In dealing with potent toxins, a methodical approach is essential, as illustrated by the history of digitalis, long recognized as a folk remedy for the symptoms of heart disease. Mentioned in herbals as early as 1250, the familiar garden foxglove (*Digitalis purpurea*) produces a mixture of about thirty glycosides, including digitoxin, diginin, and digitonin. These cardiac glycosides act directly on heart muscle in a way that is cardiotonic, functioning as a heart stimulant that improves the tone and rhythm of an ailing heartbeat.

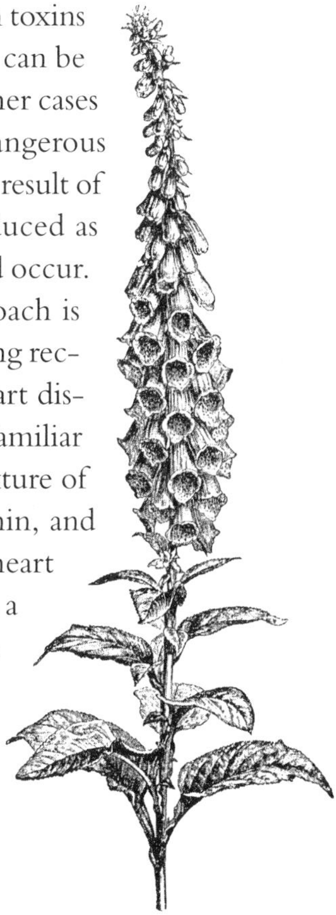

Figure 2-2. Foxglove (*Digitalis purpurea*) appeared in early herbals as a remedy for the symptoms of heart disease, and controlled doses of its cardiac glycosides have long been used to improve heartbeat tone and rhythm.

William Withering, an English country physician, determined the doses of digitalis that would be effective but not toxic. His work, published in 1758 as *An Account of the Foxglove and Some of Its Medical Uses with Practical Remarks on Dropsy and Other Diseases,* elevated foxglove from the status of a risky folk medicine to a reliable drug. Over ten years, working with only a kitchen fire and cooking pan, Withering dried foxglove leaves and painstakingly determined a safe dose of the dried product. He appreciated the value of the plant as a cure for dropsy, an old medical term for the accumulation of lymph in the body cavity, but he lacked any detailed knowledge of its chemical nature or mode of action. From a practical standpoint, Withering realized that the therapeutic dose of digitalis is alarmingly close to the toxic overdose, which is characterized by delirium, disorientation, and death. Seemingly small amounts are toxic; children have even been poisoned by chewing the flowers or tasting the nectar of foxglove flowers.

We now understand that digitalis acts as a diuretic to combat fluid retention, a symptom of heart disease. By promoting a regular heartbeat, digitalis causes more blood to reach the kidneys, where excess fluids are removed rather than accumulated in body cavities and soft tissues. The garden foxglove, while a potentially deadly species if used in unmeasured doses, has saved millions of lives in the nineteenth and twentieth centuries.

Figure 2-3. The chemistry of black nightshade (*Solanum nigrum*) varies among populations of the species; the plants can range from edible to deadly, although humans may be able to adapt to the toxic effects of the alkaloid solanine.

The determination of dose can sometimes be quite perplexing for two reasons: variations among the plants of a single species and the ability of humans over time to develop a tolerance for certain toxic compounds. The black nightshade (*Solanum nigrum*) is a cosmopolitan medicinal plant that varies in its toxicity; field guides report that some highly toxic varieties may cause death. One of black nightshade's chemical components, the alkaloid solanine, has been used as an agricultural insecticide and, when consumed, results in symptoms ranging from drowsiness and salivation to paralysis and death. Nevertheless, common nightshade has several folk uses as a treatment for tumors and cancers, eye diseases, and rabies. Curiously, despite its toxicity, nightshade is consumed as a vegetable in parts of Asia, Africa, and Europe, where it is also used in tonics for the elderly.

Traditional Asian uses of nightshade are practiced by the recent Hmong immigrants who came from the mountains of Laos to the United States and sought familiar plants in their new home. In the hills near Atlanta, Georgia, the Hmong gather nightshade to boil as a pot herb and seem immune to its various effects. Cooking helps to remove some solanine, and individuals seem to become tolerant of its ill effects as their bodies adapt to metabolize solanine. The Hmong suffer no ill effects from nightshade consumption, but the plant's ability to cause drowsiness has been exploited by other groups that do not routinely consume nightshade as part of their diet. The Rappahannock Indians steeped leaves of the related American black nightshade (*Solanum americanum*) to make a tea to treat sleeplessness. Another folk use of nightshade recalls its use as an insecticide; Kenyan tribes consume common nightshade to combat *Giardia,* a common intestinal parasite.

Gathering Information

The most abundant plants on earth are flowering plants, a diverse, dominant group that includes most known medicinal plants. While flowering plants occur worldwide and in almost all habitats, as with other groups of organisms such as birds and insects most of the diversity occurs in tropical areas. The number of plant and animal species in tropical rain forests exceeds the number of species in all other biomes combined, but tropical rain forests cover only about 7 percent of the earth's surface. Plausible explanations for this uneven distribution of species worldwide exist. Tropical habitats can support huge numbers of individuals, and competition for basic needs is rife. Plants compete for space, light, nutrients, and pollinators. Through natural selection, they evolve chemical lines of defense against attack by plant-eating insects and animals and disease-causing fungi. The long-term survivors among them are those individuals with the most potent chemical defenses and the most efficient pathways to produce these so-called secondary compounds. Their genetic legacy, as genes, is passed to the next generation of their species. Tropical habitats are diverse, and the landscape is often highly dissected, suggesting that there are many remote, defined sites that populations can colonize; small, isolated populations evolve quickly to adapt to local conditions. Growth conditions have lead to tremendous species diversity in the tropics, where species can be as distinct chemically as they may be in their vegetative forms, flowers, and fruit.

Coincidentally, as plants have responded to their predators with the evolution and perfection of potent chemical "cocktails," they have provided a vast pharmacopoeia of chemicals with potential medicinal uses for humans. These medicinal plants populate the natural ecosystems of the earth, most in their tropical habitats still awaiting discovery. In fact, very few tropical plants have been studied as extensively as opium poppy and foxglove, both temperate medicinal species. Well-known medicinal species account for less than one-half percent of flowering plants. A vast reservoir of chemically unstudied plants remains, but these plants are not really "unknown" (no more than North America was "unknown" before the arrival of European explorers). Many such plants are well understood by indigenous peoples and their healers, who have expert practical knowledge of local plants and their uses.

Many plant species remain completely unfamiliar to Western science and medicine; these species have not been collected, preserved as herbarium specimens, classified, named, and studied in laboratories for the presence of medicinal secondary compounds. Some of them may be so-called sibling species, organisms that physically may resemble each other but are genetically distinct populations that no longer interbreed. Approximately 120 prescription drugs are derived from plants, and these drugs come from only 95 plant species. Nevertheless, plant species disappear with alarming regularity, often before we learn about their medicinal potential; some botanists estimate that between 50 and 150 plant species may become extinct each day. Most of these are unrecorded, unstudied tropical plants, at least from the viewpoint of Western science and medicine.

Botanists and natural product chemists are now faced with a choice of how to proceed with further studies of tropical plants for their medicinal uses. Under ideal conditions, habitats would not be disappearing, extinction would not be an issue, and screening projects could proceed methodically in temperate and tropical sites. But with extinction a reality, how do we select species to study for their potential medicinal uses? As an analogy, imagine a vast collection of potentially valuable history books stored in a library that is burning, each text unique but lacking a title and index. How would a historian select which books to rescue and save for future study? Similar decisions must be made now about which tropical forest plants to screen for antibiotic, antiviral, chemotherapeutic, and psychoactive properties. Each unknown plant species is essentially an untitled, unread book with vast genetic and medical potential encoded in its cells.

In selecting new plants for medicinal screening, the ethnobotanical approach involves tapping into the vast store of practical knowledge that has been accumulated by shamans and other medical practitioners in tropical regions. In this method of gathering information about new drug plants, Western botanists in effect apprentice themselves to indigenous healers, working with them closely to learn local medicinal practices that might suggest new plants for laboratory study. The ethnobotanical approach to learning about medicinal plants reverses the traditional flow of information; the ethic in the past has been to bring Western medicine to cultures perceived as undeveloped. Ethnobotanists know that most of the world's inhabitants depend on folk medicine to provide effective care for everything from viral infections and cancers to childbirth. We have much to learn from indigenous people worldwide.

Another approach to drug discovery involves the broad screening of plants in habitats that support a diverse flora. The National Cancer Institute began random screening of plant extracts for anticancer activity in the 1960s, and the Pacific yew (*Taxus brevifolia*) was among the first plants examined. The recent discovery of the antitumor drug paclitaxel (taxol) from the bark and needles of this tree resulted from the random medicinal screening of plants from the Pacific Northwest. Since then paclitaxel has proven effective against human malignancies such as breast and ovarian cancers that have not responded to earlier types of chemotherapy.

The Pacific yew, a species native from the Pacific Northwest south into montane regions of Mexico, was used for venereal diseases by the Potawatomi Indians, while the Chippewa and Iroquois used the steam from boiling branches for arthritic pain. West Coast Indians used the wood for paddles and bows, and a related European species was known to the Greeks and Romans as a poisonous plant with morbid associations. Nothing indicates that Pacific yew was ever used as a cancer therapy, however, proving that random screening can yield impressive results. Unfortunately, the random medicinal screening of plants, region by region through floristically diverse areas, is time-consuming. In tropical areas, the threats of habitat destruction and species extinction require that researchers seek more efficient means of discovering new plant medicines.

The ethnobotanical approach provides researchers with "educated guesses," working hypotheses, as medicinal information from indigenous people. When distant populations are using the same or similar plants for identical uses (such as curare plants throughout the Amazon region), the evidence for their effectiveness is particularly compelling. These clues point the way to new discoveries. The plants known to Don Elijio Panti, a Mayan healer in Belize, have been recorded by Rosita Arvigo and Gregory Shropshire of the Ix Chel Tropical Research Foundation. Recently, crude extracts of several of Panti's most potent plants were examined for anti-HIV activity, yielding four times as many positive results in preliminary tests than specimens randomly selected for testing. Of course, not every new medicinal plant yields marketable medicines; some active principles prove less potent or identical to compounds already in use, while others are too toxic to be used safely as human medicines.

Ethnobotanists make decisions that affect the success of the search for new medicines. More drugs are known to people who have inhabited an area for many years, especially a region in which there is a great diversity of indigenous plants. The plants serve as a natural pharmacy in which local healers have spent years observing, collecting, studying, and preparing the species that are their primary medicines. Information is usually passed down through generations of healers, including knowledge of the most effective plant-derived drugs and their safe preparation and those plants that are too toxic for routine use. Healers often possess information that is not commonly known, knowledge of plant medicines important for treating rare or serious diseases or conditions.

The general population encounters such universal problems as contraception, childhood illnesses, and minor wounds and knows which plants to use for common ailments and treatments. Women frequently provide more accurate information about cures for reproductive complaints and pediatric problems than their male counterparts, even specialized healers. A healer would be prepared to treat more rare, potentially dangerous conditions such as viral infections, cancers, or diabetes. In Belize, healers have general medical practices and specialties such as snakebite or childbirth. They may be familiar with the medicinal uses and preparation of a hundred or more plants, information that has been passed orally through generations. For this reason Mark Plotkin, an ethnobotanist who trained with

Richard Evans Schultes at Harvard University, has likened the death
of one shaman or healer to the destruction of an entire library of
practical medical information.

Ethnobotanists in the field seek out healers and tribal chiefs and
request local and government permission to study and collect in a
particular area. They learn local languages, observe customs, and col-
laborate with local scientists. Following consultations with local healers, plants are collected. Four or five specimens of the fresh material
are pressed and mounted for herbarium collections; these serve as
reference specimens (vouchers) if there is a question about the plant's
identity. About two pounds of plant material are also preserved for
chemical analysis, either by drying or storage in a solution of water
and alcohol. Eventually, chemists in natural products laboratories at
universities, pharmaceutical companies, or government agencies
extract and analyze the secondary compounds present in the plant
material. Testing for bioactivity follows, such as the potential of some
plant drugs to halt the copying of DNA in retroviruses (such as HIV)
by interfering with the function of a specific viral enzyme. Investigators at the National Cancer Institute observe the effect of extracted
plant molecules on sixty human tumor cell lines to assess potential
anticancer activity, while other laboratories focus on new antimalarial compounds or antibiotics to fight bacterial infections.

The methods of ethnobotany have evolved remarkably in the last
half of the twentieth century. Richard Evans Schultes has recorded
almost two thousand plants used medicinally by Indians in the
northwest Amazon; he accomplished this work by living among
Indian tribes and sharing their culture and knowledge through years
of field work. His work stands in contrast to the efforts of another
hero, Joseph Rock (1884–1962), credited with bringing a botanical
cure for Hansen's disease (leprosy) to the Hawaiian Islands. Rock
traveled to Burma (now Myanmar) in search of the botanical source
of chaulmoogra oil, the kalaw tree (*Taraktogenos*), which was mentioned in the herbal of the Chinese emperor Shen Nung and later in
the Indian *Rig Veda*. As a botanist and Chinese lexicographer, Rock

was prepared for challenges that he might encounter and which he described in an early *National Geographic* article "Hunting the Chaulmoogra Tree" (March, 1922). Although he began his hunt for chaulmoogra with ethnobotanical clues as a guide, his contempt for his Burmese hosts is revealed in his description of a local healer as "a village quack" and the many "coolies" who "marched through dale and over hill for a mere pittance" to carry his supplies. The records do not mention that Rock consulted with local healers to learn more about Chinese folk medicine or sought local permission to collect the large quantities of chaulmoogra seeds that his party gathered near the village of Kyokta. Rock practiced neither local customs nor cultural immersion, and his methods stand in contrast to field practices of modern ethnobotanists. He encountered hardships in the form of bandits, tigers, malaria, and treacherous terrain and yet managed despite almost insurmountable odds to bring back the seeds that provided the first real cure for leprosy. Methods and attitudes aside, Rock brought back a plant for Western medicine that alleviated years of human fear, disfigurement, isolation, and suffering. With this initial seed stock, Hawaiian plantations were started to provide the chaulmoogra oil that would cure lepers incarcerated at Kalaupapa and elsewhere. Rock traveled to Burma only about two decades before Schultes began his field work in the northwest Amazon, but philosophically Rock was not an ethnobotanist. Schultes is considered the "father of ethnobotany," willing to live among indigenous peoples, and his methods are carried on by several of his students who continue to broaden our wider knowledge of plant medicines from remote sites in the Amazon and Pacific regions.

Herbarium Collections

An herbarium is a collection of plant specimens, pressed and dried, affixed to paper sheets and preserved for reference and study. With at least 250,000 species of flowering plants on earth adapted to diverse living conditions, it is impossible to maintain a living reference collection that would include more than a small fraction of all known species, but in many ways, herbarium collections can replace living collections. Plants that have been pressed and dried with care can preserve excellent structural detail and can be kept indefinitely if they are protected from fire, moisture, and insects. Herbaria have been made since the sixteenth century, attributed originally to Luca Ghini (1490?–1556), a botanist at Bologna whose students carried the practice throughout Europe. Early collections were mostly of medicinal species and were bound and stored vertically as shelf books, but Linnaeus later mounted plants on unbound sheets that he stored in horizontal piles, the method that is now practiced in herbarium collections worldwide. Herbaria now range from personal collections of a few hundred specimens to institutional collections of several million, including the herbarium at the Royal Botanic Gardens, Kew; the United States National Herbarium; and the herbaria at Harvard University. The specimens are arranged by genus and family in large cases; the order of the families is specified by one of the various classification systems that are in use.

The reported number of herbarium specimens worldwide is well over 273 million, although the number may be higher. These specimens can provide a tremendous resource for botanical study. Each sheet has a label that should bear the following information: the name of the collector, the number of the collection (the specimens collected by one field botanist over a lifetime are numbered sequentially), the location and date of the collection, along with anecdotal information that might include the habitat and growing conditions of the plant, habit and size, colors of flowers and fruit, along with local names and local uses of the plant. Although they may lack the physical appeal of living plants, dried specimens can be used in many similar ways: for research on floral and vegetative form, study of anatomy and development, and chemical analysis (including testing for the presence of medicinal compounds).

Field botanists rarely prepare a single herbarium sheet. Rather, one collection number is assigned to a set of four or five sheets of plant specimens that were removed either from one tree or from herbaceous plants growing closely together, to avoid mixing similar species in one collection. These sheets are then distributed and placed in several herbaria as part of their general collection, available for reference by researchers worldwide. Ethnobotanists now collect, prepare, and deposit voucher specimens for all their collections in herbaria. If an extract from one of these species later shows great promise as a botanical medicine, there will be no confusion about the natural habitat of the species and its true identity and classification.

Centuries ago, herbaria were begun principally to serve as collections of medicinal plants, and the labels still frequently include information about ethnobotanical uses of plants. As recently as the nineteenth century, many botanists were also physicians and as a matter of course recorded medicinal uses on herbarium labels, a practice that continues today. As records of botanical field work, herbaria have useful information to reveal, but only if investigators begin to read the anecdotal information that is included on many specimen labels.

Besides medicinal uses in the strict sense, other notations may reveal potential as a drug; plants that are poisonous, aromatic, irritating to skin, or used in rituals or magic may all contain quantities of potent secondary compounds. When she examined the anecdotal notes on 2.5 million herbarium sheets in the Harvard University herbaria, Siri von Reis recorded almost six thousand labels that cite medicinal properties. More than five thousand medicinal species representing nearly two thousand genera can be found in these herbaria. Certain families such as the spurges (Euphorbiaceae) and the mints (Labiatae) had high numbers of medicinal species, and the search suggested several potential new food plants as well. Herbarium specimens of the kukui tree (*Aleurites moluccana;* Plate 4), a spurge relative carried by early voyagers to the Hawaiian Islands and other tropical sites, reveal several medicinal uses; the flowers, fruit, and bark have been used for asthma, sores and ulcers, exhaustion, uterine problems, and constipation. The seeds are edible, and the oil pressed from the seeds can be used in lamps. Hawaiian species of *Pisonia* are used against thrush infections, while *hoawa* (*Pittosporum* spp.) is used to stun fish in rivers, treat sores, and ease the pain of childbirth. These species synthesize concentrated quantities of chemicals with medicinal potential. Few medicinal uses gleaned from herbarium notes have been investigated by Western medicine, but ethnobotanists have estimated that perhaps about half the folk uses of medicinal plants are valid. The potential for discovering new drug plants among herbarium records is high; a review of specimen labels at a large herbarium can yield thousands of suggestions for future investigations.

Hunting for medicinal plants in the herbarium is frequently less frustrating than searching accounts of exploration, anthropological records, herbals, or floras for medicinal plants unknown to Western medicine. In early written sources, medicinal plants are often mentioned, but without a scientific name a plant can be impossible to identify. As mentioned in the last chapter, several plants in the Badianus herbal cannot be positively identified; Aztec plant names translate as "greatly honored tree" and "blue medicine," and their illustrations also provide no suggestion of their identities. Floras, which are scientific treatises on the vegetation of a particular region, frequently make no mention of medicinal plants, and anthropologists have just recently begun citing voucher specimens of plants with local uses so that positive plant identifications are possible. Herbarium specimens provide the actual plant labeled with its identity, range, and ethnobotanical uses.

Healing Gardens

Foxglove, with its tall flower stalks and striking inflorescences, was probably first known as a garden plant, until someone sampled its leaves and assessed the practical effects of its glycosides on human heart muscle. Perhaps an elderly gardener swollen with dropsy first nibbled a foxglove flower and noted its medicinal effects. Inconspicuous herbs like the various mints were probably cultivated because they are strongly aromatic and could be used with impunity for soothing teas. Historically, gardens in which medicinal species could be cultivated provided a reliable source of plants used for treating various ailments; convenient access to medicinal plants led to more frequent use and greater familiarity with the practical aspects of medicinal chemistry and determination of dose.

European physic gardens were originally walled monastery gardens in which medicinal plants were grown for use and study, but the concept of a physic garden soon broadened to include all gardens in which medicinal plants were grown for study and observation. The first physic garden in England began at Oxford in 1621 on five meadow acres near Magdalen College to cultivate "divers simples for the advancement of the faculty of medicine." By 1648, the keeper of the garden at Oxford listed in its catalog about sixteen hundred species and varieties of native and imported plants. During the early nineteenth century, the old physic garden evolved into the botanic garden of Oxford University, but the oldest surviving botanic gardens are in Italy at Pisa (1543), Florence (1545), and Padua (1545). The new plant species that were brought back by travelers and explorers were cultivated in botanic gardens and physic gardens, whether or not they had known medicinal uses.

In 1673, the Worshipful Society of Apothecaries in the City of London began the most historically significant physic garden on a small plot on the banks of the Thames River in Chelsea. Members of the Society were able to study medicinal plants and undertake botanical experiments within the four walls of the Chelsea Physic Garden. The garden was originally laid out in plots arranged for study rather than aesthetics, although the landscape also included specimen trees. The document that in 1722 conveyed ownership of the land from Hans Sloane to the Society stipulated that each year "fifty specimens or samples of distinct plants well dried and preserved and which grew in the said garden the same year together with their respective names" would be given to the Royal Society "untill the compleat number of two thousand plants have been delivered." Now more than thirty-seven hundred specimens from this garden are in the herbarium at the Natural History Museum, London, where they provide a valuable resource of information about plants that were grown in the eighteenth century.

Philip Miller (1691–1771), author of the *Gardener's Dictionary,* was the curator of the Chelsea Physic Garden in the mid-eighteenth century, when many plants new to science were introduced into the garden. During Miller's tenure, the garden became the best supplied botanic garden in the world with exotic new plants introduced each year. Tropical species were grown in the glass houses. One such tropical introduction was grown from unknown seeds obtained from the Jardin des Plantes in Paris in 1757; the Madagascar periwinkle was named *Vinca rosea* in 1759 by Linnaeus, but it is now placed in the genus *Catharanthus* (*C. roseus*). The periwinkle traveled from the garden at Chelsea to many tropical sites worldwide, through the reciprocal seed exchanges that have been offered since the garden was founded. The periwinkle became known in Jamaica as a folk cure for diabetes, but is now valued in chemotherapy to treat Hodgkin's disease and leukemia. When eventually tested in 1949, the periwinkle seemed to have no effect on blood sugar levels, but its extracts caused the death of white blood cells in laboratory rabbits, suggesting its possible application in cancer therapy. The periwinkle is chemically among the best-known flowering plants; the leaves produce more than sixty alkaloids, including the two that are commonly used in chemotherapy, vincristine and vinblastine. The Chelsea Physic Garden now includes five thousand species, primarily plants of pharmaceutical interest, and serves as a garden for study and observation, and as a site for experimental research.

In the tropics, physic gardens also serve as plant sources and study sites. In some cases, the "garden" is not planted in the strict sense but rather exists as a natural semi-cultivated area in which the plants are known, recorded, observed, and protected. Rosita Arvigo maintains the Panti Mayan Medicine Trail in Belize, a partially cleared high bush site at which several plants used by the Mayan doctor and priest Don Elijio Panti can be studied in their natural habitat. In *Tales of a*

Shaman's Apprentice, Mark Plotkin describes his visit to a knowledgeable Creole healer while he was doing field work in French Guiana; what at first glance appeared to be a tangled "weed patch" was actually a physic garden in the most practical sense. Her garden of medicinal plants included species used for everything from liver complaints to skin lesions and toothache. Shamans also cultivate medicinal plants in forest plots, including some varieties that are not normally found in nature; essentially, chemical selection is occurring, with medicinal needs dictating which mutant forms are selected from nature for long-term cultivation as part of the tradition of local medicine. In African countries where most of the population is routinely treated by traditional healers using plant extracts, home gardens often include medicinal species.

In tropical areas where biodiversity is threatened by habitat dis-

Figure 2-4. The Chelsea Physic Garden (seen here in 1795) was an eighteenth-century hub for new botanical introductions, including the Madagascar periwinkle (*Catharanthus roseus*), source of the alkaloids vincristine and vinblastine used to treat Hodgkin's disease and leukemia.

ruption, new gardens of medicinal plants may provide the future prototype for medicinal botany. More than one thousand medicinal species are cultivated at the Sachamama Ethnobotanical Garden in Amazonian Peru, a modern physic garden that serves as a study site and as a refuge for species that are becoming increasingly rare in nature. Increased knowledge of medicinal plants is impossible if species disappear, and the loss of ethnobotanical knowledge is directly linked to the loss of local medicinal flora. As plants vanish from the landscape, traditional teaching and healing will also cease. In chapter 9, we will investigate the conservation of medicinal plants and medicinal knowledge in greater detail. If knowledge of traditional healing and the significant plants can be preserved, the outlook for medicinal botany will be bright.

CHAPTER 3

Medicinal Plants in Nature

ALMOST any habitat includes some indigenous plant species that have been used medicinally. However they are used by humans, whether to control blood pressure or cancer, the medicinal compounds produced by plants are evolutionary defense strategies in a natural world colonized by organisms competing for survival. Fumbling with an aspirin container, who contemplates the sources of salicin and salicylic acid, bucolic riverbank willows or a field of meadowsweet? Similarly, a Peruvian Indian racked with malaria does not consider the rain forest ecology and conservation of cinchona. Although most of the world's population is familiar with medicinal plants growing in their natural habitats, in Western medicine patients and professionals are accustomed to obtaining medicinal plant compounds from bottles and packets. Sterile packaging is far removed from the natural settings in which the source plants of many drugs first appeared, survived, and evolved the chemical pathways that led to medicinal secondary compounds. Imagine the surprise of visiting a cardiologist or oncologist and being given a potted seedling and some oral instructions for its cultivation and use! In Western countries we lose touch with medicinal plants in their most basic form: the whole plant. Among the world's wider population,

80 percent depend on folk medicine for healing and routinely collect, handle, and prepare wild plants.

Sacred Groves

Although medicinal species frequently disappear from ecosystems as a result of overcollection or habitat destruction, some entire forest habitats have become protected sites because of the intrinsic value of their medicinal plants. Such conserved forested habitats occur across Asia in India, Sri Lanka, China, Thailand, and Myanmar (formerly Burma); the sacred grove in Perumbavoor, in the Indian state of Kerala, is a remnant of the original virgin forest in the midst of urban sprawl. The Indian Ayurvedic system of medicine relies strongly on medicinal herbs to treat illnesses, and plants mentioned in the *Rig Veda* thrive in these sacred groves. Temples in sacred groves are used for daily worship, and the sites have become forest preserves where medicine and religion, pragmatic and spiritual forces, combine their efforts to provide protection of an ancient habitat.

Sacred groves in China provide emergency supplies of medicinal plants should a species disappear from other habitats, but they are also places for spiritual retreat, natural renewal, and preservation of native wildlife. Sacred areas are refuges where species can survive despite habitat destruction, and they exist as a result of Buddhism and not government legislation. Among the most ancient living trees, *Ginkgo biloba* may owe its survival to sacred forests near Buddhist temples; trees similar to the modern ginkgos predated the dinosaurs and existed worldwide during the Mesozoic era. China is the last home of living individuals of the genus *Ginkgo,* where the trees were a surviving remnant of the forests that once bordered the Yangtze River valley, but the trees growing today in Chinese forests may be the offspring of cultivated trees rather than wild descendants. *Ginkgo* may have survived in China because of its protected status in wooded groves near Buddhist temples, but now it thrives as a widely cultivated urban "survivor species" known for its resistance to insect pests, fungi, poor soil, and pollution.

Folk medicine has helped to preserve ancient forests because of the intrinsic value of the plants as cures and their associations with religion and magic. *Ginkgo* has long been valued as a medicinal plant, and this may have contributed to its survival as a plant in sacred areas. It was first mentioned about three thousand years ago by Shen Nung in the *Pen Tsao* and later in Lan Mao's *Dian Nan Ben Cao* as an external treatment for freckles and sores, but modern Chinese physicians use *Ginkgo* extracts for coughs and asthma and as a brain stimulant. This usage may have suggested the current European use of *Ginkgo* to treat symptoms of old age, from memory loss to arthritis. It is an interesting coincidence that an ancient tree, which probably survived near-extinction through human intervention, can be used to promote human well-being in old age. Leaf extracts containing the active ginkgolide compounds are now obtained from cultivated plantations in France and South Carolina. Very few species on earth have continued virtually unchanged since the Mesozoic era; *Ginkgo* quietly survived hundreds of millions of years in undisturbed forest habitats, until its recent revival as an urban ornamental and shade tree and source of valued medicinal compounds.

Remnants of forests in Sierra Leone support the growth of a wide medicinal flora. Many of these plants have a wide distribution in Sierra Leone, but with widespread deforestation some species can now be found only in sacred groves. Indigenous people cannot afford antibiotics or other pharmaceutical drugs and rely on the effective botanical remedies known to practitioners of folk medicine, in turn putting pressure on wild populations of medicinal plants. A plant known locally as *gbelo wuli* (*Enantia polycis*) is used com-

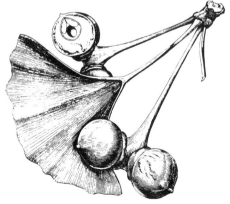

Figure 3-1. Ancestors of modern ginkgo trees (*Ginkgo biloba*) grew worldwide during the Mesozoic, and the species may have survived until modern times in protected forests near Buddhist temples.

monly for treating malaria, jaundice, and ulcers and now is uncommon, even in the sacred groves that are maintained by knowledgeable local herbalists. Medicinal plant mixtures are also important in traditional healing. Members of the Kpaa Mende tribe in southwestern Sierra Leone prepare several medicines by combining two or more plants from sacred groves. Uterine pain associated with childbirth is treated with a cooked soup of tropical yams (*Dioscorea* spp.), which produce steroidal precursors of hormones, and of cayenne pepper (*Capsicum annuum*). Other medicinal combinations are used to treat conditions ranging from schistosomiasis and scabies to venereal disease and infertility.

The surviving sacred groves form a fragmented mosaic of habitats for native plants and animals. These protected forests are small sites, usually no larger than twenty-five acres, embedded in a landscape of agricultural and pasture lands. Sacred groves also serve as sites for ceremonies and rituals, as well as botanic gardens for training local herbalists, sources of medicinal plants, and outdoor hospitals where treatments can be administered close to their source. Overuse of plant resources is prevented by a system of sanctions and taboos, but as habitats become increasing fragmented and remote, the likelihood of extinction increases even if plants and animals are not overcollected.

Medicinal Forests

Forest ecosystems are pharmaceutical factories, the sources of chemicals that prolong and save lives, but sometimes these habitats are not regarded as the nonrenewable resources that they may be. Framework trees can succumb to fire and flood, parasitic fungi, climatic change, and human activity. Perhaps because forests are large and vast, they appear to be deceptively resistant to change, buffered from human impact, and capable of infinite renewal and propagation. Forests may be resilient because of the diversity of species, and if one type of plant disappears, another often replaces it over time. Tree species can disappear as a result of disease, as in the case of the once-common American chestnut (*Castanea dentata*). The chestnut was dominant in many North American forests, with individual trees often one hundred feet or more in height, and the protein-rich chestnuts were a valuable food for humans and animals. Native Americans and early European settlers used chestnut tea to treat pertussis, and the astringent bark was a common treatment for wounds and sores, but during the twentieth century chestnut has succumbed to a parasitic fungus (*Cryphonectria parasitica*) that was accidentally introduced with nursery stock from northern China in 1904. Seedlings of other forest species have filled in the gaps left by the disappearance of the American chestnut, and mature chestnut trees have essentially disappeared from American forests, except for occasional specimens in western states. Root systems have survived and develop offshoots, which invariably are attacked by the fungus before they are able to flower and fruit.

Value as a medicinal plant can also jeopardize a species in nature. During the eighteenth century, feverbark or cinchona (*Cinchona* spp.) was nearly eradicated from tropical forests by overcollection. Cinchona is the source of the quinine used to treat malaria, a widespread parasitic disease caused by various species of *Plasmodium* protozoa. In their high-altitude habitats on the Andean slopes, the trees are widely dispersed among several other species that are adapted to growth in tropical montane habitats. The distribution of Andean trees is characteristic of other tropical forests: although the total number of different kinds of trees is high (high diversity), the number of individuals of any one tree species is low (low frequency). In other words, cinchona trees were already relatively uncommon before they were collected for quinine. This distribution pattern differs from that of trees in temperate forests, where most species are common within their habitats.

The early Jesuits in Peru taught the Indians to plant five new cinchona trees for each one that was felled and stripped of its bark. Their prudent method was to plant the seedlings in the shape of a cross, producing clusters of the mature trees as a way to replace cinchona in the forest and to thank God for an important medicine. By the 1800s, such conservation practices were abandoned, and international greed determined the rate of cinchona collection from Andean forests. The supply of remaining trees was alarmingly low, which concerned the Dutch and British governments since their colonists needed an effective medicine to combat malaria in tropical regions. Local Andean peoples guarded the remaining cinchona trees, and in an early effort to preserve forest biodiversity and their international quinine monopoly, governments in Bolivia, Peru, Colombia, and Ecuador made it illegal to export cinchona trees or seeds.

Not all cinchona trees produce equal concentrations of quinine, suggesting natural genetic variation among populations. Plants from the Lake Titicaca region of Peru were known to have particularly high chemical yields, and eventually the Dutch obtained a pound of the valuable seeds from that area to begin cinchona cultivation in Java. During the nineteenth century, Dutch horticulturists improved on nature; they experimented with selection and grafting, attaching scions with high quinine yields to root stocks with good growth. In the 1940s, a new high-yielding species (*Cinchona ledgeriana*) was discovered among the surviving trees in the Lake Titicaca region.

Herbaceous medicinal plants can also be eradicated from their natural habits through overcollection, as with the ginseng (*Panax*) that was once common in North America and Asia. Ginseng roots have been valued in Asia as a panacea for

Figure 3-2. Feverbark trees such as *Cinchona cordifolia* are the source of quinine, used by Andean Indians to treat malarial infections.

more than five thousand years; the gnarled, branched tap root suggests to some a human form, resulting in the notion that the plant must be a good treatment for all human ills. Once common in moist eastern woodlands, the American ginseng (*P. quinquefolius;* Plate 22) was gathered from the wild for export after the Asian species (*P. ginseng*) became rare. Most natural populations of native ginseng disappeared from forests in Asia and later North America from overcollection to supply the Asian ginseng market. Native Americans and European settlers gathered thousands of wild plants from forests in the Maritime Provinces south to the Appalachians and Blue Ridge. Growers attempted cultivation once most ginseng populations in America disappeared from nature, and today ginseng is field-grown in Wisconsin for export to Asia.

With a new medicinal discovery, the status of a plant can change overnight. For many years, loggers in the Pacific Northwest cut and burned the slow-growing Pacific yew trees (*Taxus brevifolia*) that are now known as the original source of the valuable anticancer drug paclitaxel (taxol). Pacific yew grows as an understory tree in the same old-growth forests of Washington and Oregon that are inhabited by the endangered spotted owl. The trees were considered worthless to the timber industry, and their taxol molecules were unknown; possibly 90 percent of the trees were destroyed before the species was recognized as synthesizing a potential cure for breast and ovarian cancers.

In North America the most diverse wooded ecosystems are the cove hardwood forests of the southern Appalachians, which are populated by forty or more tree species, with twenty to thirty woody species occurring in any one cove. These ancient habitats have existed in the Appalachians since the Tertiary period; species like the American chestnut have come and gone, but the resilient cove forests have continued intact. Most of the trees are deciduous, and the common species include basswood (*Tilia americana*), sugar maple (*Acer saccharum*), silverbell (*Halesia monticola*), tulip tree (*Liriodendron tulipifera*), beech (*Fagus grandifolia*), yellow birch (*Betula lutea*), hemlock (*Tsuga canadensis*), cucumber magnolia (*Magnolia acuminata*), red oak

(*Quercus borealis*), sweet buckeye (*Aesculus octandra*), and white ash (*Fraxinus americana*). Usually six to eight species dominate in one stand, but the forests are remarkably diverse in the number of woody plants that they support.

The deciduous tree canopy yields a rich stratum of leaf humus that enriches the forest floor, supporting a diverse layer of herbaceous ferns and wildflowers. Various trilliums (*Trillium* spp.), toothwort (*Dentaria diphylla*), trout lily (*Erythronium americanum*), Dutchman's breeches (*Dicentra cucullaria*), bloodroot (*Sanguinaria canadensis*), and hepatica (*Hepatica acutiloba*) flower in the early spring before shade blankets the forest floor. Wildflowers and ferns form an herbaceous carpet, punctuated by trees that grow tall and straight in the competition for light. Rich soils and seventy inches of annual rainfall support high rates of plant growth, and many tree species achieve their maximum size in these southern forests. The rich botanical diversity is the result of glaciation in the Pleistocene epoch; southern forests served as refuges for the northern species that dispersed in front of the encroaching ice sheets. Subsequently cove hardwood forests have served as a center of dispersal from which seeds and fruits can reach other regions. Following glaciation, the Northeast was repopulated by the descendants of plants that had "over-wintered" for millions of years in southern cove forests.

In a practical sense, the Native Americans and later the European settlers in the Appalachian cove forests found themselves in a remarkable habitat. The forest yielded edible fruits and nuts, maple syrup and sugar, wood, cordage fibers, tannins for leather, dyes for cloth and wool, and nectar for honeybees. Disease and injury could also be treated with supplies from the forest; the cove hardwood forests of the southern Appalachians are coincidentally natural pharmacies stocked with plants that produce a wide range of useful medicinal compounds. Native Americans and European settlers used hepatica (*Hepatica acutiloba*) for liver complaints and other ailments. It became a popular remedy nationwide, and 250 tons of the dried leaves were consumed in 1883 alone. Native Americans used basswood (*Tilia americana*) to make a bark tea for lung ailments, a leaf tea to treat nervous complaints, and a poultice to draw out infections of the skin. The peppery roots of toothwort (*Dentaria diphylla*) were chewed as a folk remedy for toothache, and a root poultice was applied to cure headaches. Alum root (*Heuchera americana*) had uses similar to alum, as a styptic and astringent to treat wounds. Redbud (*Cercis canadensis*) was a folk remedy for leukemia, and bark tea made from persimmon trees (*Diospyros virginiana*) was used to cure thrush. Native Americans and European settlers developed a rich tradition of folk medicine using native plants, the same species that still inhabit the ecologically diverse habitats of North America. The relationship between biodiversity and ethnobotany is not limited to tropical lands; there were virtually no diseases or conditions that could not be treated with either a tree or wildflower from the diverse native Appalachian flora. Often we think that botanical medicines must originate in rain forests, but temperate habitats also reveal new avenues for medicinal exploration and a rich source of plant compounds that await laboratory testing.

The Asian Connection

We know that *Ginkgo* trees once occurred across the Northern Hemisphere, since fossils of their leaves have been found in North America, Alaska, England, and Japan. Several genera of flowering plants, many not nearly as ancient as *Ginkgo,* show a similar pattern of geographic distribution with close species growing in eastern North America and eastern Asia. For some groups, such as the magnolias, fossils have been found in Greenland and Europe, although the plants no longer grow there as part of the modern native flora. The American and Asian representatives of a genus can belong to remarkably similar species; ginseng is one example, with Asian and American plants that are very similar in their growth forms and medicinally interchangeable.

During the eighteenth century, Carl Linnaeus noted the similarity between the floras of eastern Asia and eastern North America; his students sent back to Sweden thousands of specimens from both continents for classification and study, and no doubt he was struck by the similarities among the collections. We now know about 120 genera in which closely related species occur in eastern Asia and eastern North America, in habitats separated by distance and ocean waters. Examples include trees and shrubs such as maple (*Acer*), hickory (*Carya*), dogwood (*Cornus*), silverbell (*Halesia*), catalpa (*Bignonia*), tulip tree (*Liriodendron*), witch-hazel (*Hamamelis*), black gum (*Nyssa*), barberry (*Berberis*), as well as *Magnolia, Rhododendron, Viburnum, Stewartia,* and *Gordonia*. Several familiar North American medicinal wildflowers including jack-in-the-pulpit (*Arisaema*), blue cohosh (*Caulophyllum*), May apple (*Podophyllum*), mayflower (*Epigaea*), wild ginger (*Asarum*), and Indian pipe (*Monotropa*) have very similar Asian counterparts. Nonflowering species with Asian-American patterns of distribution include maidenhair fern (*Adiantum*) and walking fern (*Camptosorus*).

Plant geographers consider these plants to show disjunctions in their distribution, large gaps that resulted when many European species disappeared during the Pleistocene epoch. In the Northern Hemisphere, disjunct genera abound, and in some areas of Japan, China, and Korea the forests closely resemble their ecological counterparts in New England and the southern Appalachians. Several medicinal species such as ginseng occur in Asian and American forests and are included in the broad list of plants with disjunct distributions.

The American botanist Asa Gray discussed the similarity of Asian and American floras with Charles Darwin during their correspondence in the 1850s. Darwin was clearly intrigued and peppered his letters with questions about the botanical relationships between the United States and Japan. Perhaps as a result, Gray demonstrated statistically that the flora of New England more closely resembled that of Asia than Europe or even the American West. He wrote in 1859, "It would be almost impossible to avoid the conclusion that there has been a peculiar intermingling of the eastern American and eastern Asian floras, which demands explanation." He postulated that Old and New World plants had dispersed over land bridges connecting Alaska to Siberia, but we now have a more modern explanation for similar Asian and American floras. Plate tectonics and the current understanding of continental drift offer a geological explanation for plant distribution in the Northern Hemisphere.

Originally the continents formed a single supercontinent that began to break apart more than 200 million years ago into northern and southern land masses. Laurasia, the northern supercontinent, shared a common flora; forests similar to those in New England and Japan covered all the land in the Northern Hemisphere. Fossils from Greenland, Alaska, Europe, and Siberia reveal evidence of these early forests. Even when Laurasia broke apart into North America and Eurasia, the land masses were close enough for many years to allow easy exchange of fruits and seeds through animal migrations and wind. Climatic change eliminated many types of plants from western North America and Europe, but the ancient forest types still survive in eastern North America and eastern Asia. Glaciation destroyed vegetation in northeastern North America, but the forests have reformed from the many plant survivors that colonized the Appalachians. The high diversity of plant life in the Appalachians is explained by the effects of glaciation on plant distribution; northern plants that dispersed in front of the glacier commingled with southern species in the cove hardwood forests.

Several examples reveal the medicinal similarities between eastern Asian and eastern North American floras, and now we can understand the biological basis of these close relationships, the result of common ancestry between modern American and Asian species descended from plants that once blanketed Laurasia. The genus *Podophyllum* is valued medicinally on both continents; the Hindus have used the Himalayan May apple (*P. emodi*) since ancient times as a purgative and to cure skin ailments, and the Penobscot Indians of Maine relied on the May apple in New England (*P. peltatum;* Plate

23) to cure cancers. The plant became known to early settlers as the American mandrake because of its similar taproot structure and was used for hepatitis and syphilis. May apple resin (podophyllin) is used now to treat warts, and a semi-synthetic derivative (epipodophyllo-toxin) is used in treating lung and testicular cancers. Jack-in-the-pulpit (*Arisaema triphyllum*) was used by Native American tribes in poultices to treat ringworm, skin infections, arthritis, and swelling from snakebite. Its Asian counterparts are also used in India and China for snakebite, and all the species are extremely irritating because of the calcium oxalate crystals contained in the fresh leaves and underground stem. Tea made from magnolia bark was con-sumed in China as a tonic (*Magnolia officinalis*) and in North Amer-ica for malaria and typhoid fever (*M. acuminata* and *M. virginiana*). Wild ginger (*Asarum* spp.) has survived in Europe as well as in North America and Asia and has similar uses in all areas of its range. Native American tribes brewed a root tea of the American wild ginger (*A. canadense*) to treat colds and uterine problems; the Asian species (*A. balansae* in Vietnam and *A. blumei* in China and Japan) are used for identical ailments. *Aesculus,* the genus that includes horse chestnuts and buckeyes, has survived in Europe, Asia, and North America. An Asian species (*A. chinensis*) and two American buckeyes (*A. pavia* and *A. arguta*) have been used to stun fish. Extracts of *A. indica* (Plate 3) from India and the European horse chestnut (*A. hippocastanum*) have been used to treat rheumatism, and several *Aesculus* species are used as remedies for varicose veins, hemorrhoids, and sores.

Many species cultivated in North America as ornamental plants have an Asian origin; they thrive in our climate because of the simi-lar latitudes of their original Asian habitats. When they were intro-duced as garden plants, their ancient medicinal uses were forgotten, but in some cases they are clearly related to their wild American coun-terparts. The native American angelica (*Angelica atropurpurea*) and the cultivated garden angelica from Korea (*A. gigas*) have historically been used to treat female reproductive disorders. American beautyberry (*Callicarpa americana*) was used by Native Americans to treat infections and dysentery, while its Chinese relative (*C. bodinieri*) was used to treat flu symptoms in children. This example illustrates a common theme in ethnobotany: Indigenous populations experiment independently with their native plants across their natural range and frequently discover similar medicinal uses that reflect a common chemical legacy.

Dispersal and Naturalization of Medicinal Plants

When travelers prepare for a trip, they pack what they will need; their satchels might include medicines, especially if they plan to immigrate to a new land. In this way, many medicinal plants have been carried worldwide, possibly since ancient times, and some of these valued species have escaped from cultivation and become part of the local wild flora. Some plants were literally lifesavers that were carried along on all voyages and destined to be established in new homes. When early Polynesians set out into the Pacific, they brought along taro (*Colocasia antiquorum;* Plate 14), which they could use as a staple food and a versatile medicinal plant. The underground stems could be baked and then pounded into a starchy paste or dried for storage in case of famine. The green leaves provided a vegetable for steaming, and the cut petioles were rubbed on insect stings. Taro juice was sipped for fevers, the stems were rubbed on wounds to stop bleeding, and a poultice of cooked taro paste was applied to infected sores. Originally native to southeastern Asia, taro now grows wild throughout the Pacific Islands and Polynesia, western Africa, and the West Indies. It was deliberately introduced and cultivated by early arrivals who wanted taro to use for food and medicine in their new homes.

Candlenut tree or kukui (*Aleurites moluccana*) probably originated in Southeast Asia, but now occurs commonly as a naturalized species in Brazil and the West Indies. Early Polynesians carried the tree seeds to Hawaii and other Pacific Islands, where candlenut, like taro, became a plant with versatile uses. The seeds yield an oil that was burned in lamps, the bark and shell pigments dyed cloth and skin, and the juice from immature nuts was applied to babies' mouths to treat thrush. Hawaiian Islanders used the sap of the tree to prepare a medicinal drink and combined candlenut oil with the tissue of a calabash to treat skin diseases. A tea made from the spore-producing whisk fern (*Psilotum nudum*) was also used to treat thrush and other skin ailments, as well as intestinal disorders. Whisk ferns may have been carried in early Pacific migrations, but they may also have a naturally wide range. They have been variably interpreted as "living fossils," possible descendants of the first Silurian period land plants, or as advanced ferns in which the fronds have been reduced to naked branches bearing three-parted spore cases. Hawaiian Islanders used another spore-producing plant with a wide tropical distribution, the nodding clubmoss (*Lycopodium cernuum*), to make a soothing water bath to treat arthritis.

Temperate plants can also find themselves transplanted, naturalized, and thriving in the tropics. Nontoxic strains of the ubiquitous black nightshade (*Solanum nigrum*) were introduced to the Hawaiian Islands, and the plants, known locally as *popolo,* have escaped into the wild where they thrive in clearings and disturbed sites. The leaves were cooked and consumed as a vegetable during famine, and the plant yielded medicines for sore throats, coughs, digestive problems, and tonics. The variable Hawaiian plants are classified in the same species as the toxic strains of black nightshades of Europe and America, and some of these plants were used medicinally. Although black nightshade probably originated in Europe, the plant has become cosmopolitan as people have traveled and carried its seeds with them.

New World Introductions

With waves of Pilgrims, colonists, and early settlers, many European plants native to Old World forests, fields, hedgerows, and gardens were transplanted to American soils. Some plants were introduced by chance, probably the result of their small seeds being carried in with straw bedding, grain, or food supplies. On the other hand, many medicinal plants were intentional introductions, and the plants selected to make the voyage across the Atlantic were based on the tradition of herbal medicine in Europe. Once in the New World, they began in gardens, but many medicinal plants escaped from cultivation almost immediately upon their arrival. The temperate climate and soils were such that they could grow, reproduce, and disperse independently, and many herbs were aggressive growers, capable of colonizing roadsides, fields, and disturbed areas. A list of roadside plants in New England reveals several that are not native to North America, including weedy plants that arrived as part of a medicinal seed stock carried in by a practical early immigrant.

St. John's wort (*Hypericum perforatum*) was introduced from Europe to seventeenth-century New England gardens to treat ulcers, burns, sciatica, worms, melancholy, and madness. Now naturalized throughout most of the temperate United States, it grows as a perennial in dry, gravelly soil and colonizes abandoned urban lots, where it spreads with short vegetative runners. One plant can produce thirty thousand seeds in a growing season, and the seeds are light and easily carried by the wind to new areas. A less aggressive plant, the European celandine poppy (*Chelidonium majus;* Plate 12), was considered valuable for restoring eyesight, curing jaundice and ringworm, and relieving toothache. Its abundant bright yellow juice probably suggested its early use for jaundice, and female birds were believed to use celandine poppies to restore the eyesight of their fledglings whose eyes were pecked. Now the plants have spread from early New England medicinal cultivation to moist sites aside gardens, farms, woodlands, and roads.

The common roadside tansy (*Tanacetum vulgare;* Plate 27) was used as a weak leaf tea for dyspepsia, worms, kidney ailments, and digestion, although its essential oils are now recognized as potentially lethal. It was also used to repel insects and preserve corpses and meat. Another roadside weed, chicory (*Cichorium intybus*), began in the New World as a cure for jaundice and other liver complaints, while the invasive wetland species purple loosestrife (*Lythrum salicaria*) was introduced as a medicinal plant to treat wounds, ulcers, and blindness. Purple loosestrife is now an environmental scourge in several states, where it colonizes and blankets wetlands, altering habitats by drying up standing water and competing with native plants for territory and nutrients.

American lawns also reveal their complement of early European medicinal plants. Self heal (*Prunella vulgaris*) was used to treat wounds, and the broad-leaved plantain (*Plantago major*) had similar applications, as well as being considered a cure for jaundice and kidney complaints. Shepherd's purse (*Capsella bursa-pastoris*) was mixed into an ointment for head wounds and was used to treat ear ailments and toothache. Bugleweed (*Ajuga reptans*) was prepared in syrups and plasters, and the herbalists Gerard and Culpepper recommended it for preventing "inward burstings" and dissolving blood clots. Ground ivy (*Glechoma hederacea;* Plate 18) was regarded as a panacea by the early herbalists, so no wonder it was included in New World gardens of useful herbs. Now naturalized as a common weed in American lawns, it was once revered as a cure for headaches, wounds, kidney ailments, and mental illness. A collection of household recipes and cures from 1746 enjoins "good wives, tender mothers, and careful nurses" to boil handfuls of the plant in white wine, mix them with oil, and rub this ointment into the shaved head of a lunatic to effect a cure.

Nineteenth-century gardeners also included medicinal plants among the plants grown for practical uses. In *The American Gardener's Calendar* (1806), Bernard M'Mahon listed several European and Asian species as "Plants Cultivated for Medicinal Purposes," including some that have now escaped from cultivation and have naturalized in wild habitats. Among these were foxglove (*Digitalis purpurea*), poison hemlock (*Conium maculatum*), stinging nettles (*Urtica urens*), catnip (*Nepeta cataria*), flax (*Linum usitatissimum*), comfrey (*Symphytum officinale;* Plate 26), and the opium poppy (*Papaver somniferum*), which were cultivated to be used in the sickroom, although some were probably prized in the garden for their form and color as well. In the first edition of *The Frugal American Housewife* (1829), Lydia Maria Child also recommended growing medicinal herbs for general household use. Her list of such plants included traditional European herbs along with some native North American species such as maidenhair fern (*Adiantum pedatum;* Plate 2) for coughs and American pennyroyal (*Hedeoma pulegioides*) for digestive disorders. Both these species were used by Native Americans for various ailments and could be easily cultivated in American gardens. Her text mentions a tea made with motherwort (*Leonurus cardiaca*) as "quieting to the nerves" and for "students and other people troubled with wakefulness." Originally introduced from Eurasia as a medicinal plant useful for heart ailments and childbirth, motherwort was eventually adopted by the Algonquin Indians to treat female reproductive problems. Motherwort is now naturalized throughout most of the United States, from the northeastern to the western states, suggesting its widespread use and cultivation during the nineteenth century.

The exchange between the Old World and New World of medicinal plants and herbal knowledge began with the first European settlers on the American continent and is now reflected by many plants that inhabit our landscape. By the mid-nineteenth century, the result was an American herbal tradition that incorporated and combined aspects of European and Native American knowledge of diseases, medicinal plants, and effective cures. For instance, in *The Indian Household Medicine Guide* (1882) J. I. Lighthall revealed the Native American uses of many North

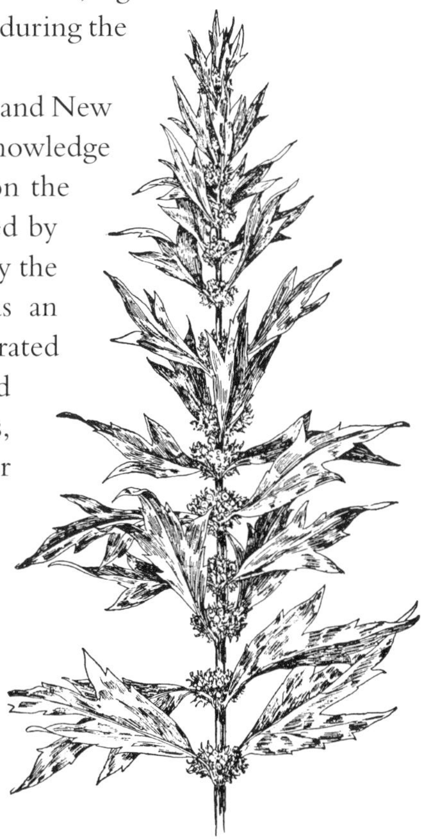

Figure 3-3. Motherwort (*Leonurus cardiaca*), a Eurasian species now naturalized in the United States, became a popular nineteenth-century treatment for female reproductive ailments and the symptoms of childbirth.

American plants that could be useful to physicians in treating their patients. He advocated "the Indian herbal theory," which included using native plants such as skunk cabbage (*Symplocarpus foetidus*) to treat tuberculosis and sassafras (*Sassafras albidum*) to purify the blood. Lighthall also mentioned Native American uses of introduced European plants such as mullein (*Verbascum thapsus*) for coughs and hops (*Humulus lupulus*) to induce sleep, illustrating the commingled medicinal floras of Native Americans and European settlers.

Curiosity, Cultivation, and History

The active ingredients of medicinal plants are secondary compounds that evolved in plants competing to survive in nature. Human curiosity, awareness, and experimentation revealed medicinal properties and earned these plants the privileges of cultivation and protection. Seeds were saved and carried worldwide. The healing that began with foraging continued with foresight in gardens of medicinal plants, sometimes far from the native habitats where medicinal species first grew. Gardens were the most reliable source of medicinal plants, serving as living pharmacies that could provide at short notice medicinal compounds for illness, discomfort, old age, or childbirth.

Some medicinal plants have escaped from gardens back into the wild, not always growing where they first evolved, which reflects the history and extent of their use. Other species have nearly disappeared from nature because of human demand and greed, regardless of the politics of biodiversity and the implications of plant extinction. Herb plots are fashionable today in Western gardens, but householders are more likely to use snippets for the table than to brew a decoction to fight an ear infection. Few in our culture would rely on a knot garden to supply a family's pharmaceutical needs, but we recall that medicinal herbs were brought into cultivation from the wild for serious reasons, in some cases matters of life and death.

Some medicinal plants are still cultivated in many old southern gardens, in what seems an unbroken relationship with such household species as the opium poppy (*Papaver somniferum*) and castor bean (*Ricinus communis*). Opium poppies originated in Asia, and the castor bean is a tropical introduction; one cures pain, and the other combats constipation. They are regarded as essential garden plants by many, even though presumably no one is using them now to harvest opium or press castor oil. Both are naturalized and can be found self-sowing and surviving in nature, but more significantly, they are among the plants that are passed around from gardener to gardener to be grown in vernacular gardens. Their history is medicinal, and their lore is historical.

We have come full circle in our expectations, anticipating daily botanical discoveries of medicinal significance in the rain forest, while growing heirloom species in herb gardens with no expectation other than aromatic pleasure. Plants with medicinal potential surround us, some indigenous and others introduced by our forebears. Our understanding of medical science and medicinal botany remains incomplete, a vast field that requires appreciation of nature and the human condition.

CHAPTER 4

~

Toxins and Cures:
A Cabinet of Plant Chemicals

A QUIET forest grove can be a biological battleground. Plant-eating animals select specimens to devour, while trees synthesize a chemical arsenal stashed in their succulent green leaves, bark, or roots. Even ephemeral wildflowers rooted in the forest floor join in the subtle mayhem. A plant that appears to be a suitable meal can repel, sicken, confuse, stunt, sterilize, or kill a hungry animal that consumes it if the plant produces toxins. Some plants can also wage warfare for territory by releasing into the soil toxins that discourage the growth of seedlings of other species. Their armament at the microbial level includes compounds that inhibit soil bacteria and fungi, major agents of plant disease. This chemical arsenal is apparently necessary for survival on land; relatively few aquatic plants produce compounds that deter plant-eating animals.

When plants first colonized land during the Silurian period, they were probably eminently edible, but the gradual evolution of terrestrial animals jeopardized their survival. Photosynthesizing plants are the starting point for energy flow in terrestrial ecosystems; they convert the energy from sunlight to energy-rich sugars, which are available for their use and as food for animals and decomposers such as bacteria and fungi. Various insects, amphibians, reptiles, birds, and mammals all relied on plants as food sources and were capable of doing considerable harm to plant bodies. The adaptations of plant-eating dinosaurs alone illustrate the evolutionary pressures to exploit land plants as a food source. The jaws of conifer-eating hadrosaurs produced rows of hundreds of sharp teeth, which could be replaced as they wore down from grinding the tough needles. Some plant-eating dinosaurs even employed outside mechanical help; they swallowed stones that helped to grind tough ingested leaves into a digestible pulp. The botanical ability to fight back against plant-eaters with chemical deterrents and toxins became an integral part of life on land for many plant species. Different groups have evolved various metabolic pathways to synthesize so-called phytochemicals (the Greek word *phyto* means "plant"), all of them natural products and some of them extremely dangerous.

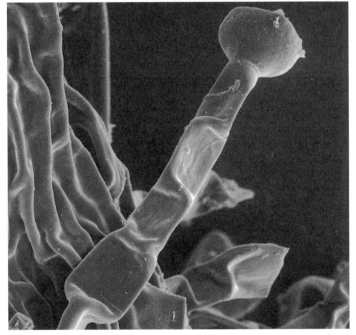

Figure 4-1. The secondary compounds of *Pittosporum oligodontum* are produced in multicellular trichomes that cover the surface of the plant (scanning electron micrograph, 750×).

This explanation for the diversity of natural plant chemistry has not always been accepted. For years, plant compounds were considered a fortunate accident of nature, perhaps the by-products of cellular metabolism that accumulated as toxic wastes in living tissues. Unlike the chemicals involved in basic metabolism, these were deemed "secondary compounds," a vast array of miscellaneous chemicals that could be found in the tissues of certain plant species. Some are specific to a single type of plant or family, and none seem to be essential to the fundamental processes of photosynthesis, cell growth, and maintenance. In short, they seemed to be superfluous biochemical by-products that accumulated in plant cells; these compounds were considered of no use to the plants, but in some cases they became useful medicines for a variety of human ills. Worldwide, since ancient times, most effective medicines were derived from plants, and today almost half of all prescription drugs in the United States contain one of more components with botanical origins, not a bad track record for biological "wastes."

With increased knowledge of plant chemistry during the nineteenth century, the list of known noxious phytochemicals grew to include tannins, terpenoids, alkaloids, glycosides, essential oils, pyrethrins, phytoalexins, organic acids, and various crystals. These compounds are in the cytoplasm of living cells, impregnated in the cell walls of nonliving wood and bark cells, or packaged in epidermal plant hairs (trichomes) that can coat vulnerable stems and leaves.

A Natural Explanation

In the 1950s, Gottfried Fraenkel considered an alternative theory to explain the presence of secondary compounds in plants. He knew that a satisfactory explanation had never been offered. Were secondary compounds really waste products of cellular metabolism? Not all plants produce them. Furthermore, the existence of secondary compounds was frequently correlated with evolutionary lines and systems of classification; certain botanical families, subfamilies, genera, and species were known for their chemical potency. It seemed unlikely to Fraenkel that secondary compounds had anything to do with basic metabolism and growth. On the other hand, as an entomologist, he was acutely aware of the damage that plant-eating insects could render to plants in nature and in cultivation. In "The Raison d'Être of Secondary Plant Compounds," an article published in *Science* in 1959, he suggested that secondary compounds arose to protect plants from plant-eating predators. He noted that most insects are highly selective in their eating habits and speculated, "We must assume that early in their evolution plants developed the characteristics which made them unpalatable to the rising multitude of insects. The unpalatability was accomplished by the production of a vast array of chemical compounds."

Fraenkel realized that many plant-eating insects had "learned" in an evolutionary sense to recognize food plants by their secondary compounds. In some cases, insect species had developed the ability to metabolize the secondary compounds that had evolved to prevent insects from feeding! Members of the mustard family (Cruciferae) can be recognized by the mustard oils that originally evolved to protect them; caterpillars of white cabbage butterflies find heads of cabbage and other cultivated and wild mustards based on their chemical rather than physical traits. Caterpillars of the diamondback moth also feed on mustards, but they can be deceived by entomologists armed with test tubes of mustard compounds such as sinigrin and sinalbin. If plants from other families are first anointed with mustard oils, the caterpillars recognize them as food and enjoy a full meal. Similar examples occur in celery (*Apium cepa*) and several of its relatives, in which the essential oils flag the plants for consumption by the caterpillars of swallowtail butterflies. Secondary compounds can thus become a liability in nature for plants; unfortunately, the plants under siege are saddled with the genes that keep them synthesizing their distinguishing chemical markers. Mustard oils from the Cruciferae and essential oils from the Umbelliferae have been used as human medicines, but that has no significance in the natural world where plants must defend themselves from vegetarian predators. Over time and many generations we can anticipate some new evolutionary responses from these plants to counteract devious insect-feeding strategies.

Family Histories

The Cruciferae (mustard family) and Umbelliferae (parsley family) are on a short list of very old flowering plant families, not because of their evolutionary past but because they have been recognized as natural groups for centuries by physicians and botanists. Mustards and umbellifers were used medicinally long before their secondary compounds were studied in the laboratory. Their chemistry has been recognized in a practical way since ancient times, and their original family names reflect this early knowledge in a subtle way: Palmae (palms), Gramineae (grasses), Cruciferae (mustards), Leguminosae (legumes), Guttiferae (garcinias, mangosteens), Umbelliferae (parsley), Labiatae (mints), and Compositae (daisies, sunflowers).

These names remain in use because they are applied to old families, natural groups that botanists recognized long before there were international agreements about plant names. Today rules govern the coining of plant names, as set forth in the *International Code of Botanical Nomenclature*. Family names now end in the suffix *-aceae*. Each older (pre-*Code*) family also has a more recent name with the conventional *-aceae* ending; the Cruciferae can also be called the Brassicaceae, while the Apiaceae is an alternate name for members of the Umbelliferae. It is not a coincidence that these early families are among the most easily recognizable clusters of related species with similar physical and chemical characteristics.

The mustards and umbellifers have unique chemical properties, as do the members of the mint family (Labiatae or Lamiaceae), which produce their characteristic pungent oils concentrated in epidermal trichomes. Mints can often be recognized in the field or garden by rubbing or crushing their hairy leaves to release a characteristic scent.

A practical understanding of such family chemistry is nothing new; a 1699 commentary by James Petiver, an English botanist and apothecary, noted that within the "Herbae Umbelliferae," as well as in the mustards and mints, similar species "have the like virtue and tendency to work the same effects." Similar chemical properties are also seen in many garcinias (Guttiferae or Clusiaceae), a large family that includes the tropical mangosteens (the source of various gums, resins, and pigments) and medicinal plants such as St. John's wort (*Hypericum* spp.). Compounds from St. John's wort have been used to treat mental disorders for centuries, and the plants also produce the red flavonoid pigments that are characteristic of woody, tropical genera of Guttiferae.

Notable chemical traits occur in other old families. Toxicity occurs frequently in the legume family (Leguminosae or Fabaceae), in which several species are marked by the presence of poisonous alkaloids, but it seems more likely that the family was originally recognized by similarities in flower and fruit structure throughout its seven hundred genera rather than by chemical traits. The complex mixtures of essential oils found in members of the daisy family (Compositae or Asteraceae) such as chamomile (*Matricaria chamomilla*) and tansy (*Tanacetum vulgare;* Plate 27) were the chemical basis for many uses of these plants in the European herbal tradition. Grasses (Gramineae or Poaceae) have cells that contain silica deposits, which are arranged in alternating patterns with elongated epidermal cells to form the outer covering of grass plants. The characteristic texture of grasses is the result of their high silica content; while not a secondary compound in the strict sense, concentrated silica toughens grass stems and sends many plant-eating animals elsewhere.

Carbon Chemistry

Besides water and some dissolved salts, the biochemical substances that compose living organisms are based on the chemistry of carbon. Cellular molecules such as proteins, sugars, starches, fats, and DNA are built of a framework of carbon atoms that can bond to each other to form complex structures. Carbon can also bond to other elements such as oxygen, hydrogen, nitrogen, phosphorus, and sulfur, and these are also incorporated into the molecules found in living cells. A carbon atom forms four bonds with other atoms, which in turn can bond with other atoms, making carbon the ideal element to form the basic skeleton of complex molecules. Like Tinkertoys, linked carbons can take the form of single or linked rings or chains that may be branched or unbranched, depending on the compound that is being produced.

Many fundamental cellular materials may be made of repeating, smaller building-block molecules that are based on a carbon framework. Starch and cellulose are built of smaller six-carbon sugar molecules, and proteins consist of many nitrogen-containing amino acids linked into long chains. Fats have long chains of carbons and hydrogens, so-called fatty acids, which tend to repel water. The DNA molecules that control heredity are composed of smaller molecular components known as nucleotides, each consisting of a five-carbon sugar, a phosphate-containing group, and a base with one or two rings built of carbon and nitrogen. Originally, such carbon-based molecules in cells were deemed "organic" and were thought to be the exclusive products of living organisms. Organic chemistry was once considered the equivalent of cellular chemistry, but now we know that carbon-based molecules can also be made synthetically in the laboratory.

The secondary compounds produced by plants as a line of defense are also organic molecules built of carbon, hydrogen, oxygen, nitrogen, and sulfur. Their molecular structures depend upon the type of molecule being examined; for instance, alkaloids always contain nitrogen, mustard oils always include sulfur, and glycosides always have a carbon-based sugar as part of their structure. Some secondary compounds such as some alkaloids are relatively small, simple molecules, while others are larger and more complex, such as the tannins that characterize oaks. None, however, equal in molecular size and complexity some basic plant cell substances such cellulose, starch, proteins, and DNA. The structural diversity of secondary compounds reflects the evolutionary diversity of land plants; specific groups are often defined by their secondary compounds and their unique carbon-based structures. Considerably more chemical diversity is seen among secondary compounds than in more "fundamental" cellular molecules such as DNA, chlorophyll, and cellulose, which are common to all green plants.

Early Strategies

The first land plants faced challenges to their survival on *terra firma,* from desiccation in the air to mutation from the ultraviolet waves of intense sunlight. Consumption by land animals was yet another problem, but natural selection provided evolutionary strategies for survival. Land plants developed a layer of epidermal cells, coated against water loss by a waxy cuticle layer. Leaves became tough and difficult to chew, exemplified by the unpalatable cycads (Cycadaceae), steadfast Mesozoic-era survivors that outlived generations of plant-eating dinosaurs. Without water to serve as a filter for direct sunlight, ultraviolet radiation from the sun could mutate DNA, the information-storing molecules in the genes and chromosomes that control heredity. Flavonoid pigments were one early evolutionary response to the dangers of direct sunlight because their molecules reflect ultraviolet wavelengths of light.

Flavonoids are widespread in many plant groups and probably occur in all flowering plants. Structurally they are relatively simple molecules, consisting of two six-carbon rings connected by a three-carbon ring. Within cells they accumulate in the central vacuole, a large water-filled sac that can accommodate dissolved wastes, stored sugars, and pigments. One group of flavonoids, the anthocyanins, provides most of the blue, violet, and red pigments that occur in flower petals. They are water soluble and color-sensitive to changes in acidity, so that one molecular structure can provide a range of color variations depending upon the acidity of the cell vacuole where it is stored. Anthocyanins also occur in buds and leaves. The flavonols, another group of flavonoids, are white or nearly colorless and occur in leaves and flowers. They impart autumn color to tree leaves by converting to anthocyanins while also reflecting mutation-causing ultraviolet light. Another significant benefit of flavonoid chemistry is that high concentrations of these compounds render plant leaves unpalatable to predators.

Many plants also contain tannins, astringent compounds like cori-lagin that can drastically limit a plant's potential as a food source. These compounds were probably the second group of chemical deterrents to appear in land plants, and many "living fossils" such as tree ferns and cycads have high tannin concentrations. Some paleon-tologists have even suggested that the extinction of dinosaurs was the result of poisoning by tannins. Like flavonoids, tannins are solu-ble in water and are stored in the vacuoles of living cells. They are

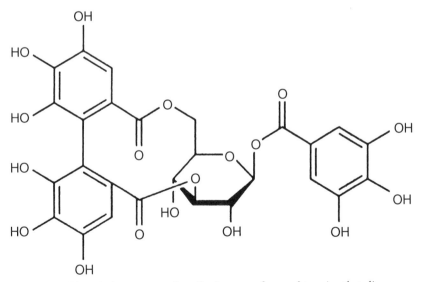

Figure 4-2. Chemical structure of corilagin, one of several tannins that discour-age browsing plant-eaters with their intensely bitter taste.

yellow or brown in color and frequently accumulate in the bark of woody species. Conifers such as redwoods (*Sequoiadendron giganteum*) and flowering plants such as oaks (*Quercus* spp.), tea (*Thea sinensis*), mahogany (*Swietenia mahogani*), and sorghum (*Sorghum bicolor*) have high tannin concentrations.

Animals often immediately reject as food plants with a high tannin content because they are extremely bitter, but there are biochemical effects as well. If an animal eats leaves containing tannins, the molecules will interfere with food breakdown by binding to digestive enzymes and to edible proteins in the plant tissues. Long-term exposure to tannins may also cause certain cancers, as suggested by high nasal sinus malignancy rates in woodworkers and artisans exposed to tannins used in the leather industry. In the Hunan Province of China, where black (high tannin) teas are consumed daily, cancer of the esophagus is relatively frequent, but the Western practice of adding milk to tea may help to alleviate the carcinogenic effects. When milk is stirred into tea, the milk protein casein binds to tannin molecules, rendering them insoluble and inactive. Similar correlations occur on Curacao in the West Indies, where a liver tonic prepared from *Krameria ixina,* a shrub with a high tannin content, seems to cause esophageal cancer in those who drink it daily.

Strains of sorghum with a high tannin content are insect-resistant in the field, but cattle raised on sorghum as fodder will grow 20 percent larger if they are fed the low tannin varieties. Native American tribes learned to soak the bitter acorns from tannin-producing oaks in water to leach away excess tannins before using the acorns as a nutritious food. As a result of natural selection, animals such as pigs, squirrels, and some woodpeckers can tolerate high tannin concentrations in their diet and consume large numbers of acorns with impunity.

Tannin concentration can vary up to 300 percent among the leaves on one tree, making foraging a challenge for caterpillars seeking food. They may need to sample several leaves before finding one suitable for safe consumption. Furthermore, while searching, caterpillars waste time and energy and possibly expose themselves to predators as they travel among leaves in the canopy. Tannins provide protection, but their production represents a tremendous energy investment for the trees; up to 30 percent of the dry weight of a sugar maple (*Acer saccharum*) leaf can consist of tannin molecules.

Terpenes and Essential Oils

The pungency of pine and spruce reveals the presence of terpenes, compounds made of carbon and hydrogen that are named for the turpentines that can be distilled from the resin of various conifers. Canals filled with the sticky terpene-laden resin run through the wood and needles of conifers where they provide the first line of defense from animal attack. As a chemical group, terpenes also include various essential oils such as limonene from citrus fruits and geraniol from roses and geraniums. Camphor, which can be distilled from the wood of a cinnamon relative (*Cinnamomum camphora*), repels insects; it is a monoterpene (a single ring structure with ten carbons) like the essential oils associated with pungency in many families. The terpene-laden essential oil in red cedar (*Juniperus virginiana*) is used to repel clothing moths in closets and trunks lined with cedar wood.

In preparing mummies, ancient Egyptians used pine and fir resins as the primary preservative to deter insect attack. The resins were spread in body cavities, on the face and body surface, on the viscera, and even over the coffin; the blackened appearance of mummies is probably the result of these resins. Resins were considered such valuable substances that they were imported from trees native to the eastern Mediterranean region. The proof of efficacy lies in the mummified remains, and insects

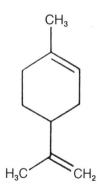

Figure 4-3. Chemical structure of limonene, the essential oil that is concentrated in the skin of citrus fruit.

have ignored these terpene-protected corpses for thousands of years. In nature, insects can sense differences in terpene concentrations. Pine-leaf scale insects can distinguish between pine trees with low and high terpene concentrations and carefully limit their feeding to trees with low terpene contents in their needles.

Azadirachtin, one of many secondary compounds produced by neem trees (*Azadirachta indica*), is a complex terpene that deters insect attack and prevents insect larvae from undergoing metamorphosis into adult forms. Neem trees also vary in their production of various secondary compounds, between populations and even from tree to tree. In tropical countries they have been used for years to protect crops, stored grains, and even library books. More than two hundred insects are deterred by neem, and in the Sudan a 1939 locust swarm devoured the leaves of all but the neem trees.

Neem compounds also act against the parasites that cause malaria and Chagas disease. Malaria continues to be a threat in Central and South America, Africa, Haiti, the Dominican Republic, and parts of Asia. More than 200 million people die from malarial infections each year, and many maternal and infant deaths are caused by quinine-resistant strains of *Plasmodium falciparum*. New botanical cures for malaria await discovery, and many may prove to be terpenes. In his 1527 treatise, the herbalist Li Shi-zen advised treating fevers with an infusion of *qing hao* leaves in water, which led to the realization that the annual wormwood (*Artemisia annua*) might kill *Plasmodium* cells. In 1972 chemists isolated artemisinin, a new terpene known only from this Asian wormwood species. The molecule is characterized by a linked pair of oxygen atoms joining two parts of the carbon framework. As the artemisinin molecule breaks apart, the paired oxygens have weak oxidizing properties (similar to hydrogen peroxide) that can destroy the outer membrane of the *Plasmodium* cells that cause malaria.

Secondary compounds with potent psychotropic effects can dangerously alter the awareness and reflexes of plant-eating animals. An example is the active ingredient of hemp or marijuana (*Cannabis sativa*), tetrahydrocannabinol (THC), a complex terpene-based compound. More than twenty related compounds have been isolated from hemp, but most of the hallucinogenic activity resides in THC. These psychoactive molecules are packaged in surface trichomes, dense hairs that discourage plant-eating animals when they begin to feed. The physiological effects of THC have the potential to linger for days or weeks, since the molecules can dissolve in cellular fats where they can persist for days before being metabolized. Hemp has been cultivated for years, and varieties grown for narcotic use have more of the active terpene than those cultivated for their fibers.

Paclitaxel (taxol), another complex terpene, was first found in Pacific yew (*Taxus brevifolia*) during a screening of North American plants by the National Cancer Institute for potential anticancer activity. It has proven useful in treating several stubborn cancers, where it acts by interfering with cell divisions using a seemingly unique mechanism. The terpene molecules bind to the microtubules in the cell that pull apart chromosomes. Paclitaxel stops the microtubules

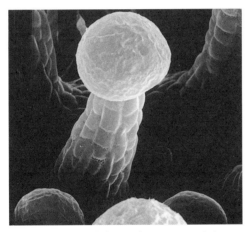

Figure 4-4. Glandular trichomes containing the compound tetrahydrocannabinol (THC) occur on the surface of hemp leaves (*Cannabis sativa*) (scanning electron micrograph, 100×). Photo courtesy of Paul Mahlberg.

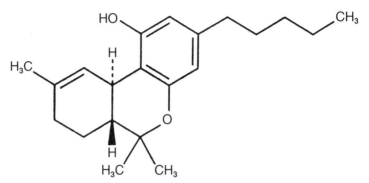

Figure 4-5. Chemical structure of tetrahydrocannabinol (THC), a hallucinogenic secondary compound in hemp (*Cannabis sativa*).

from separating the chromosomes, reforming, and repeating the division process, and in this way prevents a cancerous cell from producing generations of progeny. It halts the uncontrolled growth associated with malignancies, but can also affect division of normal cells in hair follicles or the stomach lining, for example. Presumably an animal grazing on the leaves and bark of Pacific yew would receive a dose of paclitaxel that could interfere with normal cell divisions and growth.

Terpenes have other functions besides discouraging animals from a vegetarian meal. Some plants release terpenes from their leaves or roots into the soil, where the molecules serve as toxins that inhibit the growth of other plant species. This effect is an example of allelopathy, a chemical line of defense in which plants can establish and defend territory for their growth and expansion. Black walnuts (*Juglans nigra*) release juglone from their roots, and seasoned gardeners know that this terpene inhibits the growth of herbaceous and woody plants in areas occupied by these trees. The terpenes released by the foliage of purple sage (*Salvia leucophylla*) evaporate, spread through the air, and eventually settle as toxic deposits on soil particles. Aerial photographs show a zone of clearing around sage plants where no other species can survive, surrounded by a zone of inhibition in which a few stunted herbaceous annuals grow, before terpene toxicity levels allow normal vegetation to resume. The common garden sage (*S. officinalis*) also produces essential oils containing terpenes such as thujone and cineole; these exhibit antibiotic properties and have commonly been used for throat infections, wounds, and as a tea for digestion. Overdoses of these terpenes result in dizziness, irregular heartbeat, and convulsions, which probably discourage plant-eating animals from grazing too long on sage leaves. Garden sage is a common culinary herb, but one handbook lists the toxic dose for humans as being more than half an ounce of dried leaves or "prolonged use."

Alkaloids

Many plants are bitter to taste because of the presence of alkaloids, compounds consisting of rings of carbon and nitrogen atoms that cause physiological reactions in animals. On the pH scale, which measures levels of acidity, they usually are slightly basic (alkaline), as opposed to neutral or acidic. Alkaloids are a chemically diverse group that seem to be synthesized in plant cells from amino acids, the building blocks of proteins. Perhaps one-fifth of all flowering plants contain one or more alkaloids, and more than five thousand alkaloids have been isolated. Many plant species synthesize several alkaloid molecules; besides morphine and codeine, opium poppy produces twenty-four other alkaloids. They are given names with the suffix *-ine,* for instance, caffeine, theobromine, strychnine, and cocaine. An understanding of alkaloid chemistry is important to medicine and toxicology, inasmuch as these compounds have been used as cures and poisons since ancient times.

The discovery of alkaloids is a colorful chapter in the history of chemistry that began with a basic pharmaceutical question: Why was some opium more potent than others? Opium was known to be a mixture of plant chemicals, and the only way to obtain standard doses for pain relief would require separating the components of opium.

Friedrich Wilhelm Sertürner 1783–1841) began as a young pharmaceutical apprentice and soon took on the challenge of purifying the pain-relieving compounds in opium. He extracted the crystals of a bitter alkaline substance, which he masked with sugar syrup and fed to rats, mice, cats, and dogs. Using trial and error, he worked out the doses that would put animals to sleep but not cause coma or death. In a letter written in 1803 to Professor Trommsdorff at the University of Erfurt, Sertürner described the crystals as "the specific narcotic element of opium . . . the *Principium somniferum.*" Sertürner published a paper on opium purification and kept a vial of his *Principium somniferum.* A few years later he dosed himself with the compound to relieve a terrible toothache, and the crystals worked so well that he soon sought out three young men to serve as human "guinea pigs" in experiments with his purified compound; fortunately all four did survive, despite the danger of overdose when using sufficient quantities of the compound to induce sleep. Sertürner named the alkaline substance morphine, after the Greek god of dreams, Morpheus, and pharmaceutical significance of this first-known alkaloid for relieving pain was soon recognized.

Rather than being mere deterrents to animal grazing, alkaloids are toxins that can seriously damage or poison animals that consume them. Their physiological effects range from the "alertness" associated with caffeine to the muscle paralysis and death rendered by the coniine alkaloids in the poison hemlock (*Conium maculatum*). This herbaceous hemlock, a toxic member of the parsley family (Umbelliferae) that is botanically unrelated to the coniferous hemlock tree (*Tsuga canadensis*), was used to execute the Greek philosopher Socrates. False hellebore (*Veratrum viride*) also owes its toxicity to an alkaloid, veratrine,

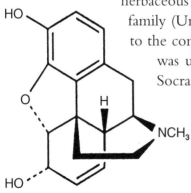

Figure 4-6. Chemical structure of morphine, one of twenty-six alkaloids produced by opium poppies (*Papaver somniferum*).

which affects heart activity. It can be deadly in uncontrolled doses (and is occasionally mistaken for an edible plant in spring), but supplies a valuable pharmaceutical medicine that controls heart rate and lowers blood pressure. Victorian garden books shared the lurid details of death by aconitine poisoning, which occurred when the underground stems of monk's-hood (*Aconitum* spp.) were mistaken for the tubers of Jerusalem artichokes (*Helianthus tuberosus*), an edible sunflower relative. *The Merck Index* describes the alkaloid aconitine as a "violent poison" and notes that it produces heart arrhythmia in laboratory animals.

Hallucinogenic species can also deter plant-eating animals, and the effects of these can be quite dramatic, as we know from human experiences. To survive predation, the risk of falling, and other natural hazards, animals must avoid ingesting chemicals that alter their senses and perceptions, so the survival value of hallucinogens for plants is clear. Besides their role in ecosystems, hallucinogenic alkaloids have been used by local cultures in religious and shamanistic ceremonies. During religious ceremonies Aztec Indians consumed the mescaline-laden "buttons" of peyote cactus (*Lophophora williamsii*), dried disks of cactus stem that cause nausea, chills, anxiety, and changes in vision. We can assume that similar physiological effects occur in peyote-grazing animals. Various Mexican members of the morning glory family (Convolvulaceae) were used by Aztec Indians for divination. These species produce strongly hallucinogenic alkaloids such as ergine; the alkaloids are chemically identical to those produced by the ergot fungus (*Calviceps purpurea*) and are derived from lysergic acid and lysergic acid amide. They cause a decrease in blood circulation, intense hallucinations, and severe convulsions and gangrene—symptoms of Saint Anthony's fire, a dreaded Medieval affliction caused by consuming grain infected with the ergot fungus. In controlled medicinal doses, ergot alkaloids can be used to treat migraine headaches and strengthen uterine contractions in childbirth. The compound LSD (D-lysergic acid diethylamide) is a laboratory-altered version of the natural alkaloid ergometrine.

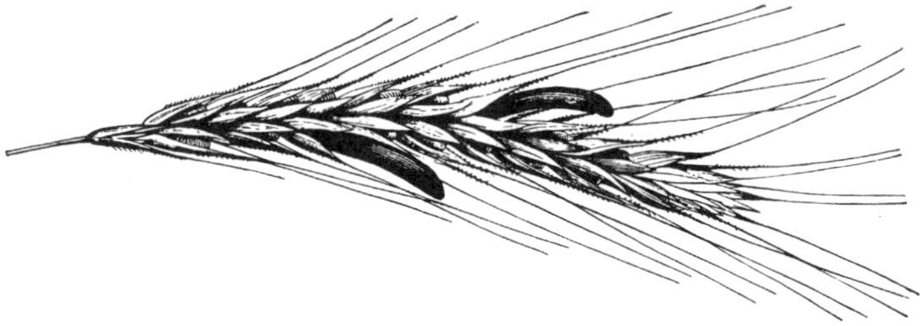

Figure 4-7. The ergot fungus (*Claviceps purpurea*) growing on rye (*Secale cereale*) caused periodic outbreaks of Saint Anthony's fire, the symptoms of severe poisoning by ergot-produced alkaloids.

Families can be characterized by their unique alkaloid chemistry. The tropane alkaloids of the tomato and potato family (Solanaceae) include atropine, scopalomine, and hyoscyamine, compounds produced in varying proportions by several genera. The amount of these potent alkaloids also varies with the plant part sampled, stage of development, weather, and even the time of day that the plant is gathered. Dry weather seems to induce synthesis of these alkaloids, and they are present in higher concentrations at night; perhaps plants were most vulnerable to attack by nocturnal predators. Scopalomine is strongly hallucinogenic, while other tropane alkaloids influence the sympathetic nervous system, heart rate, and dilation of blood vessels. This outcome suggests the effects of these compounds on plant-eating animals; probably a small sample sends them elsewhere for a meal. Atropine keeps the iris of the eye open by blocking the sphincter muscle and is now used medicinally in eye examinations. It has also been used to alleviate pain and to treat the palsy associated with Parkinson's disease. Scopalomine has been administered as a "truth serum" in criminal proceedings and mixed with morphine to alleviate the pain of childbirth through the state of "twilight sleep."

The effect of consuming a mixture of tropane alkaloids is dramatic, as recorded in Jamestown, Virginia, when hungry soldiers consumed the fruits of Jimson weed or thorn apple (*Datura stramonium*). According to a contemporary record (1705), the soldiers hallucinated for eleven days with behavior that included silliness and nudity as part of their "frantick Condition." Practical knowledge of tropane alkaloids dates from earlier in history, from Roman through Medieval times, when mixtures of tropane alkaloids provided the chemical basis for witches' brews concocted from local species in the tomato and potato family (Solanaceae). These brews were administered as salves and ointments and seem to constitute the chemical basis of witchcraft lore. As fat-soluble molecules, the tropane alkaloids can pass through the skin; such mixtures can induce the combined sensations of flying and frenzy, flights from reality that were associated with witchcraft. One seventeenth-century formula includes belladonna (*Atropa belladonna*) and henbane (*Hyoscyamus niger*), both potent sources of tropane alkaloids. Belladonna was known during the Middle Ages as devil's herb or sorcerer's herb, and although it has medical uses, it is so toxic that ingesting one berry can cause death. The genus *Atropa* was named by Linnaeus for Atropos, the Fate in Greek mythology who cuts the thread of life.

Belladonna and henbane are related to mandrake (*Mandragora officinarum*), in which the tropane alkaloids are concentrated in the large, branched taproot. Early believers in the Doctrine of Signatures imagined a human form in the taproot of mandrake and from this

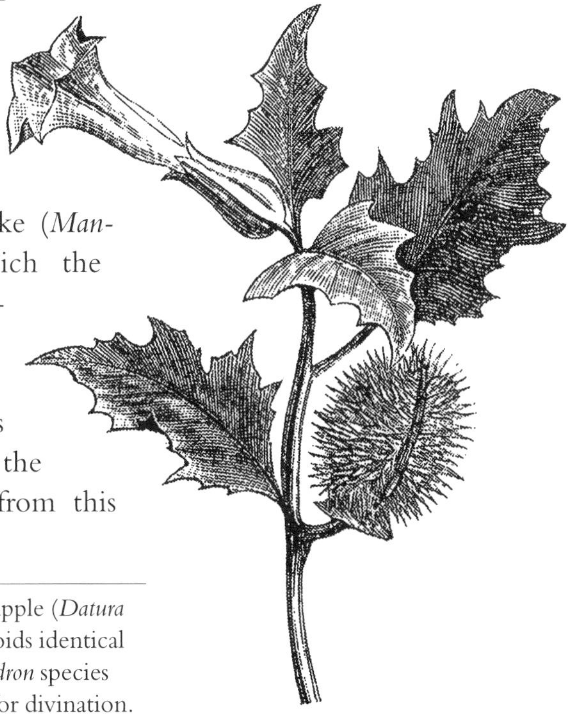

Figure 4-8. Jimson weed or thorn apple (*Datura stramonium*) produces tropane alkaloids identical to those found in the *Methysticodendron* species used by South American shamans for divination.

concluded that it is a panacea for all human complaints. Their notion had a chemical basis; mandrake produces atropine and scopolamine and was used to deaden pain two thousand years before the invention of ether. Henbane was also cultivated in Europe as a narcotic for surgery, administered as a vapor from a sponge moistened with the plant juices. Gerard's *Herball* (1597) described it as causing "an unquiet sleepe, like unto the sleepe of drunkennesse, which continueth long and is deadly to the party." Obviously, care had to be taken in its use. William Shakespeare revealed practical herbal knowledge in his plays and may have described an alkaloid-induced sleep in *Romeo and Juliet;* Friar Lawrence provides Juliet with a vial of a potent medicine to simulate her demise "stiff and stark and cold, appear like death; / And in this borrowed likeness of shrunk death / Thou shalt continue two and forty hours, / And then awake as from a pleasant sleep."

Another group of alkaloids, the glycoalkaloids, is related chemically to steroids, which include the hormones that regulate sexual development and reproduction. Glycoalkaloids are also plentiful in the tomato and potato family (Solanaceae), where they discourage animal grazers by binding to the cell membranes of the skin cells coating the mouth and tongue. The effect is extreme bitterness, and the molecules cause cell breakdown in the tissue lining the mouth and stomach of their attackers. Field studies done with the fruit of horse nettle (*Solanum carolinense*) and black nightshade (*Solanum nigrum*) show that when given a choice, animals prefer fruits with lower levels of glycoalkaloids. This preference protects immature fruit from being eaten, but glycoalkaloids may also

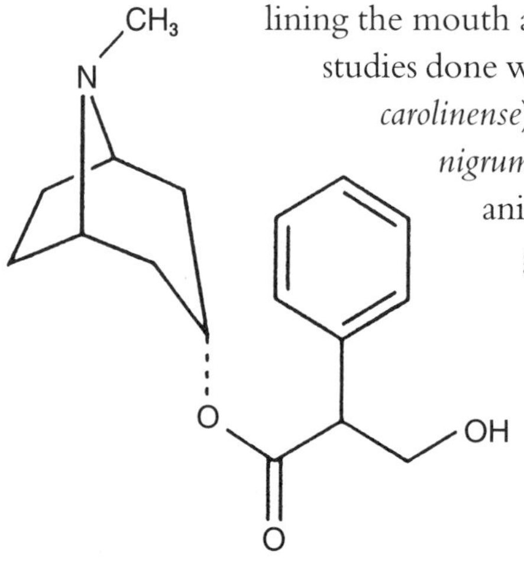

Figure 4-9. Chemical structure of atropine, a tropane alkaloid that causes delirium and agitation.

serve as a line of defense against invading fungi. Wild fruits with high concentrations of glycoalkaloids do not succumb to decomposition by fungi as easily as plants lacking these compounds. The strategy seems to involve producing a high enough concentration to inhibit fungal attack, while not entirely discouraging the birds and mammals that feed on the fruits and spread the seeds to new habitats. Glycoalkaloids are also abundant in sprouted potatoes (*Solanum tuberosum*) and unripe tomatoes (*Lycopersicon esculentum*), and there are acceptable safe limits for glycoalkaloid content in cultivated food plants whose wild ancestors developed this strategy for avoiding fungi. The glycoalkaloids in woody nightshade (*Solanum dulcamara;* Plate 25) have been used as a molecular starting point for the laboratory synthesis of medicinal alkaloids.

Besides the ecological and medical significance of toxins, alkaloid chemistry can be used in systematic botany to determine the evolutionary relationships among families. The coffee family (Rubiaceae) can be related to the dogbane (Apocynaceae) and logania (Loganiaceae) families on the strength of the complex indole alkaloids common to all three groups; these include such important medicinal compounds as vincristine, vinblastine, and reserpine, as well as the highly poisonous alkaloid strychnine. The isoquinoline alkaloids point to an evolutionary relationship among the buttercup (Ranunculaceae), barberry (Berberidaceae), and poppy (Papaveraceae) families. One approach to searching for new plant medicines takes advantage of the chemical characteristics of certain families; plants related to known medicinal species are likely candidates for screening and may themselves produce some potential new medicinal compounds.

Glycosides

Like the alkaloids, glycosides are abundant in certain families. Each molecule consists of a sugar (often the simple six-carbon glucose molecule) bonded to another nonsugar compound. The nonsugar component of a glycoside is chemically variable, depending upon the type of glycoside, and this part of the molecule is frequently toxic and often has medicinal potential. Glycosides also affect physiology, from strengthening the contraction of heart muscle to slowing the stages of animal development.

Cyanogenic glycosides such as amygdalin can produce hydrocyanic acid (HCN), a cyanide compound that is released whenever plant tissue containing it is crushed or damaged. Amygdalin is responsible for the familiar taste and scent of bitter almonds, and it occurs in the genus *Prunus* (plums, apricots, cherries, peaches, and almonds) and in other members of the rose family (Rosaceae). As HCN molecules are released through digestion, they disrupt metabolic activity in the mitochondria, the cellular bodies in which food molecules are broken apart to release energy. The cells can no longer use oxygen and suffer death as a result of cyanide poisoning. Cyanide poisoning can result in nausea, dizziness, vomiting, collapse, and respiratory failure in humans, presumably with similar effects in animals.

Early editions of the *United States Pharmacopoeia* included black cherry bark (*Prunus serotina*) and bitter almond seeds (*Prunus dulcis*), both potent sources of hydrocyanic acid when crushed. Cherokee and Iroquois Indians used infusions of cherry bark for treating colds, coughs, tuberculosis, and female reproductive problems. Regardless of its toxic qualities, amygdalin has been marketed as laetrile, an unproven cancer remedy promoted as capable of selectively destroying cancer cells by cyanide poisoning. Experimental trials with amygdalin have produced no measurable antitumor activity. Cyanide-producing glycosides also occur in cassava, a starch from tropical manioc plants (*Manihot esculenta*). "Sweet" and "bitter" varieties of manioc are recognized by their glycoside content; the tubers are rendered safe for eating by cooking or prolonged exposure to the sun, before they are pounded into starch for bread, soup, or tapioca.

Other plants produce cardiac glycosides that affect the activity of heart muscle, causing disorientation, arrhythmic contractions, seizures, and heart failure when they are consumed. These molecules are known from several genera, including foxglove (*Digitalis* spp.), squill (*Urginea* spp.), oleander (*Nerium* spp.), and milkweed (*Asclepias* spp.; Plate 6), all of which have been recognized as medicinal or poisonous, depending upon dose. Folk uses of foxglove and squill for heart ailments date back to ancient times, and these plants are still the source of cardiac glycosides like digitalin, which is used to regulate heart activity in cases of congestive heart failure. African vines in the genus *Strophanthus* were first used for arrow poisons, but now they are known to Western medicine as the source of ouabain, a cardiac glycoside with rapid effects in heart emergencies. Various milkweeds

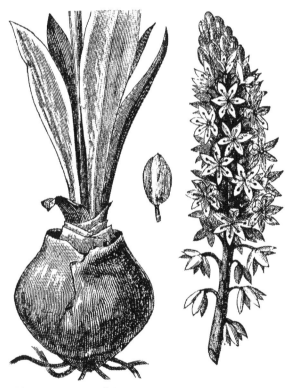

Figure 4-10. Squill (*Urginea maritima*) produces cardiac glycosides that have been used since ancient times to regulate blood pressure and treat heart failure.

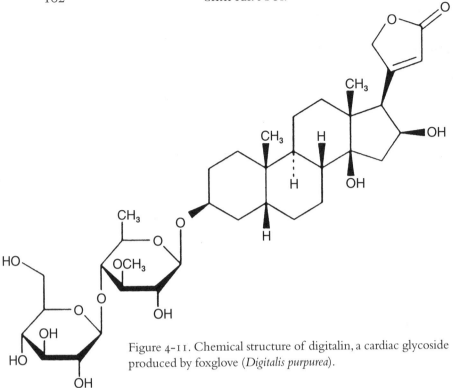

Figure 4-11. Chemical structure of digitalin, a cardiac glycoside
produced by foxglove (*Digitalis purpurea*).

also use cardiac glycosides to avoid plant-eaters, but the larvae of
monarch butterflies have evolved the ability to ingest quantities of
milkweed with impunity (Plate 7). The caterpillars concentrate the
milkweed compounds in their bodies, and the adult butterflies survive by delivering a dose of cardiac glycosides to birds that prey
upon them.

The mustard family (Cruciferae) and a few other families produce mustard oils, sulfur-containing glycosides like sinigrin that are
made in specialized myrosin cells. They yield the typical pungency
associated with wild and cultivated mustard plants like horseradish
(*Armoracia rusticana;* Plate 5), once used to make a poultice for gout
and arthritis, and they are the chemical basis of mustard plasters.
Mustards range from toothwort (*Dentaria diphylla*), which was used
by Native American tribes for colds and headaches, to field mustard

(*Brassica oleracea*), a single species that includes cultivated varieties ranging from kale and kohlrabi to broccoli, cabbage, and cauliflower. Gardeners observe that the voracious larvae of white and yellow cabbage butterflies seem to thrive on cultivated members of the mustard family. Like monarch butterflies, these insects can now graze on plants containing toxins that originally evolved as insect deterrents.

Sweet clover (*Melilotus officinalis;* Plate 20) produces coumarins, toxic glycoside molecules that can link to form dicoumarins, if the clover is stored as silage that becomes invaded by fungi. Dicoumarins are strong anticoagulants that can cause internal bleeding and death; small doses are used medicinally to break apart blood clots, while toxic doses are the basis of a commercial rodent poison (Warfarin) that causes internal bleeding and death. Smaller amounts of coumarin occur in other species, including lavender (*Lavandula officinalis*) and cinnamon (*Cinnamomum zeylandicum*). The woolly leaves of mullein (*Verbascum thapsus*) contain coumarin and the natural insecticide rotenone, which should be sufficient to discourage its traditional use as an herbal remedy for asthma, bronchitis, and kidney infections. With its thick covering of trichomes and arsenal of toxic chemicals, mullein seems particularly well protected against planteating predators.

Early settlers from Europe carried with them the seeds of another glycoside-laden species, one that could be used as a household soap substitute and folk remedy for skin ailments. Bouncing bet (*Saponaria officinalis*) was the first known source of saponins, relatively common glycosides with a wide range of properties, including the ability to foam when the crushed leaves

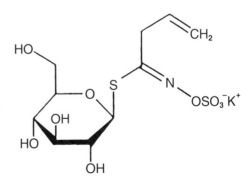

Figure 4-12. Chemical structure of sinigrin, a mustard oil, one of the sulfur-containing glycosides produced by members of the mustard family (Cruciferae).

and roots are lathered in water. Some saponins are antibiotics that apparently protect roots from soil fungi, while others inhibit the growth of human cancers and have potential as chemotherapeutic drugs. Structurally, saponins can have a terpene or a steroid bonded to a sugar molecule, which relates them chemically to the steroid-containing glycosides that interfere with insect and animal life cycles.

This last group of glycosides exerts subtle control over the life cycles of plant-eating predators. What more insidious way for a plant to combat hungry animals than by interfering with their development and life cycle? Sexual reproduction and maturation are hormone-regulated developmental milestones in insect and animal life cycles, important stages that define reproductive success. The human reproductive hormones progesterone, estrogen, and testosterone are not unique in their chemistry; they are built upon the basic plan of four carbon rings that characterizes all steroids, a group of compounds that includes both cholesterol and various insect and animal hormones. Also included here are the plant steroids, secondary plant compounds that mimic the structure and physiological action of various animal hormones.

Medical benefits of this molecular similarity are already a reality. The synthesis of cortisone and oral contraceptives from plant precursors was first based on steroids made by Mexican yams (*Dioscorea* spp.). Tropical yams should not be confused with sweet potatoes (*Ipomoea batatas*); true yams are the enlarged underground tubers of vines that have been a source of staple dietary starch for centuries, and they are the source of steroids. The molecular structure of four carbon rings isolated from yam tubers provided the original chemical starting point for the pharmaceutical synthesis of cortisone and oral contraceptives. Several species of *Dioscorea* contain sufficient concentrations of the steroid diosgenin to make them valuable sources of precursors for drug synthesis, and medicinal steroids have also been produced from soybeans (*Glycine max*), various species of *Agave* and *Yucca,* and a tropical potato relative (*Solanum aviculare*). Starting the laboratory synthesis of cortisone with plant steroids is easier and

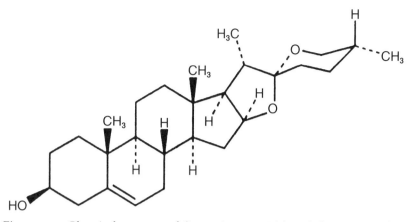

Figure 4-13. Chemical structure of diosgenin, a steroid-based glycoside produced by Mexican yams (*Dioscorea* spp.).

less costly than synthesis using the bile acids in cattle urine, which
was the method used in the first half of the twentieth century.

Oral contraceptives work by simulating the hormone levels of
pregnancy so that ovulation and fertilization do not occur. Presumably the hormone-like compounds produced by plants serve to control the reproduction of herbivorous animals that threaten plant populations by interfering with normal developmental and reproductive
stages. Plant-produced molecules that mimic the developmental
hormones of insects interfere with the normal stages of development
and reproduction by keeping young insects in a perpetually juvenile
state. Rather than simply discouraging or poisoning their animal ene-
mies, these compounds control the plant-eaters using hormonal
strategies; several examples will be discussed in the next chapter.

The Cabinet Revealed

Given the diversity, complexity, distribution, and effects of plant secondary compounds, why did biologists and chemists first overlook
their role as natural deterrents and toxins? Since ancient times, physicians, herbalists, and shamans have used phytochemicals as medi-

cines, and plants remain the single most abundant natural source of effective medicinal compounds. Yet whether in a rain forest or hospital, we are all guilty of anthropocentric thinking, assuming that plant chemicals exist exclusively for our use. When a medicinal plant produces secondary compounds that are in demand as medicines, this leads to issues of biodiversity conservation and species preservation. We once dismissed many remarkable molecules as metabolic wastes and ignored the biological significance of secondary compounds in natural habitats. The chemical strategies that were invisible for years now constitute a largely unexplored area of natural product chemistry.

Physicians are no longer botanists, and they prescribe plant chemicals as medicines based on their efficacy, regardless of their role in nature. An appreciation of ecosystems, natural selection, and survival is not necessary to practice medicine in developed countries. We should nevertheless not forget that plants invest energy and resources in producing chemicals as strategies to sustain their lives; for millions of years, natural selection has favored the chemically potent plants that survive when attacked by hungry dinosaurs, caterpillars, and moles. The array of plant compounds available for medicinal uses reflects the challenges and travails of life on earth for succulent green survivors.

CHAPTER 5

~

Defensive Strategies and Plant Chemistry

OTANICAL self-defense involves an array of munitions. Spines, thorns, prickles, epidermal hairs, waxy coatings, tough leaves, and noxious chemicals all evolved as lines of defense against hungry plant-eating animals. Despite this botanical "armor," green plants still provide a nutritional basis for ecosystems through photosynthesis. Sunlight energy captured by green plants cycles through the trophic (feeding) levels of an ecosystem, supporting other organisms ranging from insects and mollusks to vertebrates such as birds, reptiles, and mammals. Carnivores eat herbivores, so the food energy for meat-eaters comes indirectly from plants. When a tree dies and decomposes, it is attacked by fungi and other organisms that recycle its molecules and stored energy back into the ecosystem. Even soil bacteria and fungi and the various invertebrates involved in natural recycling depend ultimately on organic compounds made by green plants as their food source.

Not only do plants provide food energy for ecosystems, but the secondary plant compounds associated with chemical defense can cycle in natural ecosystems and play a significant part in the interactions among species. Insects in particular are voracious plant-eaters, and they constitute a tremendously diverse group of successful land animals. Before metamorphosing into a butterfly, a caterpillar can eat up to twenty times its dry weight in leaf tissue. As might be predicted, some plants have evolved secondary compounds that serve specifically as potent insect deterrents. A Mexican sneezeweed (*Helenium* sp.) and arnica (*Arnica montana*), both members of the daisy family (Compositae), synthesize helenalin, a lactone that serves as a powerful insect repellent. In traditional herbal medicine, arnica has been used as an external antiseptic for wounds, and helenalin also shows antitumor activity, although it is highly toxic if ingested.

Other plant-produced insecticides have been used commercially to discourage insect pests, even if they are too toxic to have potential medicinal uses. Pyrethrum daisies (*Chrysanthemum cinerariifolium*) produce pyrethrins, valued for years as deterrents to malarial mosquitoes, lice, fleas, and flies. The roots of the leguminous vine derris (*Derris elliptica*) and related species from Malaya produce rotenone in their roots, which can account for up to 20 percent of the dry weight of the root tissue. Ground derris roots have been used for centuries as an insecticide. South American cubé trees (*Lonchocarpus* spp.), also legumes, are another source of rotenone that can be used to dust agricultural crops. Local populations in the Old and New World tropics have also used derris and cubé as fish and arrow poisons, independent ethnobotanical discoveries of the toxicity of rotenone. Even the common yellow mullein (*Verbascum thapsus*), a European introduction once used to prepare a tea for bronchitis, contains rotenone in its densely hairy leaves.

Neem (*Azadirachta indica*) has long been recognized in India as a tree that naturally repels plant-eating insects and nematodes; the complex terpene-based compound known as azadirachtin protects all parts of the plant from insect attack. Neem seeds can be crushed and soaked in water overnight to produce a potent pesticide that does not harm mammals, birds, earthworms, and bees, and neem leaves buried in grain bins keep the stored crops insect-free. Unlike rotenone, however, neem compounds also have medicinal potential. Neem extracts have been used in India to treat human infections caused by viruses and fungi, suggesting that the secondary compounds produced by neem may also protect the trees from a wide range of plant diseases.

Insect Strategies

A plant may be consumed in many ways, as insects illustrate with some remarkably adaptive feeding strategies. Since Biblical times, farmers have battled migratory locusts that eat indiscriminately; locust mouthparts are adapted to chew virtually any green plant tissue available. Swarms consist of billions of insects that can consume tons of plant material in a few days, but their feeding method is essentially unspecialized. More advanced insects such as leaf miners invade the inner leaf and consume the succulent green cells between the waxy epidermal layers, while others bore deep into stems, woody trunks, and roots, where they can feed safely while hidden from predators.

Sucking insects such as leafhoppers, cicadas, and scale insects often tap directly into the conducting cells of green plants to sip water from xylem cells and sugary sap from phloem cells. The pointed mouthparts of aphids can puncture the leaf epidermis and avoid contact with surface trichomes that often contain the secondary compounds that evolved to deter plant-eating insects. By feeding so precisely, aphids also can bypass the internal cell-lined canals that contain toxic compounds, such as those that occur in parsley (*Petroselinum crispum*) and its relatives in the Umbelliferae. Other insects feed exclusively on nutrient-laden seeds and fruits, a strategy that has ominous implications for the survival of the next plant generation. Seeds in particular are a valuable source of proteins and fats and provide a nutritious diet for many insect larvae.

Some insects such as locusts and armyworms are polyphagous (literally "many-eating"), capable of feeding on several types of plants, but most insects are quite specific in their selection of foods. Insects can identify suitable plant species by their individual chemistry. Secondary compounds can serve as signals for the olfactory receptors that are often positioned on insect antennae, and a female insect seeking the ideal plant on which to deposit her cache of eggs may also examine a leaf with the chemoreceptors on her ovipositor; her maternal instinct to provide for her young may be guided by plant chemistry. Ironically, volatile compounds such as essential oils first evolved to deter plant-eaters, but some insects now use these molecules as biological markers to identify potential food sources for themselves and their offspring. The caterpillars of some swallowtail butterflies usually feed on Queen Anne's lace (*Daucus carota*) and other members of the Umbelliferae, while the larvae of cabbage butterflies thrive on cultivated and wild species of the mustard family (Cruciferae). Mustard oils attract the adult female butterflies, which in turn deposit their eggs on the leaves of various mustards, including cultivated forms of *Brassica oleracea* such as cabbage, kale, and broccoli. Mustard oils also provide a chemical feeding cue for the caterpillars of cabbage butterflies, which will ignore physical cues and try to eat filter paper that has been soaked in mustard oils. These insects are oligophagous (literally "few-feeding"), a strategy that allows them to feed specifically on certain plants with a minimum of competition from other plant-eating insects. They have also become immune to the toxic effects of mustard oils. Polyphagous insects are routinely exposed to various toxic secondary

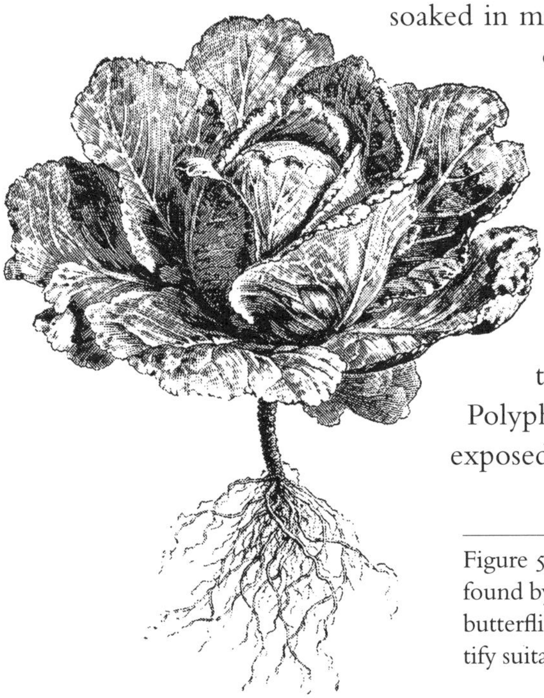

Figure 5-1. Cabbage (*Brassica oleracea*) is found by female white and yellow cabbage butterflies, which use mustard oils to identify suitable food sources for their larvae.

compounds in their broad botanical diets and have evolved bio-chemical strategies to deal with these dangers; they have high amounts of oxidases, digestive enzymes that can disarm plant toxins.

Plant Strategies

Secondary compounds are not synthesized without a cost to the plants that produce them; organic molecules require raw materials and the energy to construct these compounds by complex biochem-ical pathways. Many plants have evolved subtle mechanisms that promote the production of these protective molecules only when they are most needed. In many species, secondary compounds accu-mulate in tissues during the growing season, so that the leaves and twigs produced in early spring are more likely to be consumed by herbivores. Roots, particularly prone to subterranean grazing as well as attack by parasitic bacteria and fungi, often have the highest con-centrations of secondary compounds in the plant. It is not a coinci-dence that early Greek purveyors of medicinal herbs were known as root diggers, since the underground parts are frequently the most chemically potent part of a medicinal or toxic species. Early herbal illustrations frequently portrayed the roots and rhizomes of medic-inal plants more accurately than the leaves, flowers, and fruit, while modern botanical illustrations usually emphasize the aerial parts of a plant.

Variation in the distribution of secondary compounds in plants extends beyond season and anatomy. When gypsy moths defoliate oak trees (*Quercus* spp.), the new leaves have a higher tannin concen-tration than the original foliage; the tannin molecules bind with proteins, making plant tissues indigestible by plant-eating insects. The leaves are also tougher in texture and lower in water content, which along with the toxic tannins results in the slowed growth and development of gypsy moth caterpillars and adults. When snowshoe hares graze heavily on paper birch (*Betula papyrifera*) saplings, the new shoots that grow up from the roots produce higher concentrations of secondary compounds that will deter future feeding. When an extract made from the new toxic shoots is sprayed on edible shoots, the hares avoid them as well.

Leaves of Sitka willow (*Salix sitchensis*) damaged by insects show a decrease in their nutritional value, and this same chemical change also occurs in undamaged neighboring willows. Perhaps an airborne chemical communicates the message of impending insect attack to nearby willow trees. Potato plants (*Solanum tuberosum*) damaged by insects also increase their level of proteinase inhibitors that disrupt insect digestion and stunt their growth; one damaged leaf sends a chemical message to other leaves to synthesize greater concentrations of these protective molecules. Warning communication even occurs between plant species; the pungent leaves of sage (*Salvia* spp.) release the volatile compound methyl jasmonate when they are crushed, which in turn stimulates nearby tomato plants (*Lycopersicon esculentum*) to produce proteinase inhibitors that halt grazing insects. Mechanisms such as this suggest possible ways to induce natural insect resistance in cultivated plants.

Fruits contain the seeds that become the next generation, and their protection from herbivores before they are ready to be dispersed is important to species survival. Many examples are seen in the various red berries and stone fruits like cherries that are adapted to attract hungry birds. Birds feast on the brightly pigmented ripe fruits and later release the seeds far from the parent plant; red pigmentation is a visible cue that signals a palatable fruit with mature seeds. While the seeds are still developing, the fruit wall remains hard, green, starchy, and often laden with bitter or astringent secondary compounds. The developing fruits are protected from a wide range of herbivores and possibly pathogenic microbes, as well. A study by Betty Kreuger and Daniel Potter of the fruits of American holly (*Ilex opaca*) showed high saponin concentrations, bitter glycosides that are known to be toxic to invertebrates. Unripe berries added to insect diets slowed the growth and survival of caterpillars and deterred the feeding of Japanese beetles. Saponin levels drop as the fruits mature and redden, but a degree of chemical protection continues into maturity. Even red holly berries contain high levels of bitter tannins that inhibit insect feeding and growth, but which apparently do not deter the birds and squirrels that consume and disperse the ripe fruit.

Several plants produce secondary compounds that induce severe sensitivity to sunlight. When an armyworm (the caterpillar of a phalaenid moth) feeds on various plants of the daisy family (Compositae), along with the usual leafy nutrients it ingests polyacetylenes, compounds that become highly toxic when the larval insect is exposed to sunlight. Once the polyacetylene molecules move through the worm's gut to its surface layers, they absorb the ultraviolet wavelengths radiating from the sun, and the armyworm rapidly shrivels and dies. Insect behavior has adapted to this potential hazard; various insects known as leaf-rollers, which range from moth caterpillars to weevils and wasps, have developed the ideal strategy to avoid becoming the hapless victims of chemical warfare. They shape a leaf into a small shelter where they can feed in the shade and avoid detection by predators. If a host plant contains secondary compounds that induce photosensitivity, these have no effect because the insects feed away from ultraviolet rays in their leafy protective pocket.

Mammals may also be affected by plants that become toxic in the presence of sunlight. Buckwheat (*Fagopyrum* spp.) used as fodder induces photosensi-

Figure 5-2. The berries of American holly (*Ilex opaca*) are protected from insect damage by bitter saponins and tannins.

tivity known as fagopyrism, in which the skin forms blisters and may slough off; farmers have seen these effects when light-pigmented cattle bask in the sun after feeding on buckwheat. St. John's wort (*Hypericum* spp.) and rue (*Ruta graveolens*) can also have toxic effects in the presence of sunlight, resulting in severe photodermatitis: rashes, blisters, and skin loss. The most common secondary compounds that cause sensitivity to light are the furocoumarins, plant molecules that absorb wavelengths of ultraviolet radiation greater than 3200 angstroms. Furocoumarins are produced by several families, most notably the parsley family (Umbelliferae), the legume family (Leguminosae), and the citrus family (Rutaceae).

Natural selection results in the varying production of secondary compounds in white clover (*Trifolium repens*) and bird's-foot trefoil (*Lotus corniculatus*). Some plants have the complex cyanogenic glycosides and the enzymes necessary for releasing herbivore-deterring cyanide, and these tend to be the populations in warmer areas of Europe. In a sampling of Mediterranean white clovers, 70 to 90 percent of the plants released cyanide, while Russian clovers were rarely cyanogenic. This variation suggests that natural selection favors the production of cyanide in regions where herbivores such as snails and slugs are present through the year, as opposed to cold climates in which herbivores are controlled by harsh conditions. A similar correlation between harsh climate and the ability to generate cyanide to combat herbivores seems to occur in bird's-foot trefoil plants, although some plants seem to vary randomly throughout the growing season in their cyanogenic properties.

Many plants also use secondary compounds to establish territoriality rather than combat herbivores. Various plant molecules such as essential oils, terpenes, alkaloids, steroids, phenolic compounds, and derivatives of coumarin are toxic to their botanical competitors. Members of the walnut family (Juglandaceae) such as black walnut (*Juglans nigra*) release naphthalene glucoside from their roots into the soil, where it is converted to juglone. Juglone is known to have several biological effects, including the inhibition of seed germination and the growth of seedlings competing for space and light. Black walnuts can dramatically stall the growth of pines (*Pinus* spp.), apple trees (*Malus* spp.), rhododendrons (*Rhododendron* spp.), and even walnut (*Juglans* spp.) seedlings. In poorly drained soils, seedlings die from the accumulation of juglone in the soil, but in aerated soils bacteria break down juglone rapidly.

Hackberry (*Celtis laevigata*), sage (*Salvia* spp.), and sorghum (*Sorghum* spp.) also produce allelopathic compounds that can help to eliminate competitors, but their allelopathy may be a subtle strategy resulting in growth inhibition and seasonal variations. Purple sage plants (*Salvia leucophylla*) in California release terpenes into the atmosphere that adsorb onto soil particles, where they promote the zones of clearing and inhibition that surround sage shrubs. In a variation on the strategy of direct allelopathy, members of the heath family (Ericaceae) chemically inhibit the soil fungi that grow symbiotically with pine roots. Scotland, now colonized by heaths, was once forested by pines that were cut for fuel during the Industrial Revolution; reforestation has been thwarted by heaths that inhibit the fungi essential for pine growth.

Developmental Controls

An animal with a mouthful of alkaloid-laced leaf tissue will usually find another food source; the effect of the secondary compound is to deter grazing immediately. These strategies work for thousands of plants, but some species have evolved a strategy that extends beyond the immediate deterrent effects of most secondary compounds. Plant chemicals that regulate the life cycles and development of herbivores are more potentially controlling because their legacy affects future generations. Some plants produce molecules that mimic the hormones controlling animal reproduction and development, and they package these molecules in their leaves, stems, and roots. Among these are the steroid-containing glycosides discussed in the last chapter. Animals that eat these plants receive a dose of a defense chemical that can interfere with the normal stages of development and the production of viable young.

Insect development may follow one of two basic plans. Advanced species progress through distinct stages from eggs to larvae, pupae, and sexually mature adults. A butterfly passes through these stages as it metamorphoses from caterpillar to winged adult through a cocoon stage that encloses the developing pupa. More primitive insects exhibit a less dramatic change in their physical form; they grow by shedding their outer layers, with each new stage (instar) being larger than the one that it follows. The adults may differ from the young forms only in having functional wings, as in grasshoppers and dragonflies. As in vertebrate development, insect metamorphosis and sexual maturity are controlled by hormones, which in turn are produced in the appropriate sequence and quantity by the insect's glands. Plants have evolved various strategies to interfere with specific stages in insect development by producing chemical mimics of natural insect hormones.

Juvenile hormones maintain the larval state, and insects will remain as larvae indefinitely if they are continually exposed to high doses of these steroids. Balsam fir (*Abies balsamea*) delivers a dose of a juvenile hormone mimic to insect larvae that feed on various tree parts, a phenomenon first observed by researchers trying to raise insects in petri dishes lined with filter paper made from the wood pulp of balsam fir. The young insects did not progress through the normal stages of development as a result of continual exposure to juvabione, the balsam-produced secondary compound that keeps insect larvae from reaching sexual maturity. In this way, the trees have evolved a method to control future populations of herbivores; an insect larva that feeds on balsam has no reproductive future, and its offspring will never graze on balsam firs.

An alternative method of defense has plants exploiting the insect hormones known as ecdysteroids, which initiate the sequential stages of insect development. Many plants produce molecules that mimic the structure and effects of ecdysteroids, and these may even be more potent than the hormones synthesized by the insects themselves. The underground parts of the common polypody fern (*Polypodium virginianum*) contain up to 2 percent of phytosterols, one of the so-called phytoecdysteroids that can affect insect development. Bugle-weeds (*Ajuga remota*) are often the last remaining plants after locusts swarm over miles of Kenyan savanna; in the laboratory, several insect species reared on extracts of an African bugleweed showed serious developmental defects. In their metamorphosis from larvae to pupae, the insects grew abnormal head parts and could not eat, effects brought on by the "pseudo-hormones" in the bugleweed.

While the plant-produced mimics of juvenile hormones stall insect development, another group of plant secondary compounds causes precocious development and metamorphosis in insects. Compounds known as precocenes were first isolated from *Ageratum houstonianum,* a small blue-flowered member of the daisy family (Compositae) and now are known from several other plants. These compounds prevent normal secretion of an insect's juvenile hor-mone, and in this way they accelerate development that results in small, deformed adult insects. In some insects, precocenes may also induce sterility or a type of dormancy known as diapause. Diapause effectively shuts down normal insect development by lowering metabolic rate and stopping growth and metamorphosis.

As mentioned in the last chapter, vertebrates can also be affected by plant compounds that mimic the biological activity of estrogens. Australian sheep become infertile if they graze on wildflowers that produce hormones similar to estrogen. In the western United States, vole populations plummet as the animals graze during the late sum-mer and fall on mountain grasses that synthesize large quantities of phytoestrogens at the end of the growing season. The phytoestro-gens slow reproduction in the voles, just as the grasses are producing a new crop of seeds that need to be protected from herbivorous predators.

The phytoestrogens produced by soybeans (*Glycine max*) and other legumes are not as potent in their activity as animal estrogens or the steroids produced by plants, but they may be responsible for lower rates of osteoporosis and certain cancers in human populations that consume soy products on a daily basis. Actually three-ring flavonoid molecules rather than steroids (which have four carbon rings), these phytoestrogens may also have evolved to control the reproduction of herbivores that grazed on legumes. As flavonoids, they also function to reflect ultraviolet radiation and to deter grazing because they are unpalatable in high concentrations.

Besides producing mimics of reproductive hormones, some plants can release molecules that resemble insect pheromones, highly volatile chemicals used for communication in social insects. Wild potatoes (*Solanum berthaulthii*) release ß-farnesene, a compound that serves as an alarm pheromone for aphids. The aphids are bombarded with chemical alarm signals that they cannot ignore, and they flee from the potato plants. Seedlings of corn (*Zea mays*) emit a volatile chemical mixture when they are damaged by armyworms; this serves as a pheromone that attracts female parasitic wasps, natural predators of armyworms. The volatile molecules released by the corn seedlings include terpenoids, terpene-based compounds that also serve as deterrents to plant-eating animals. Perhaps the most devious strategies that have evolved to rid plants of their insect predators are those that involve releasing hormone-like and pheromone-like molecules.

Borrowed Molecules

We know that some insects eat plants with potent secondary compounds, but they are immune to the effects of these toxins. Instead, the plant-produced molecules can accumulate in the insects' bodies, being transferred from larval to mature forms as development progresses. Children and animals alike know the brown liquid that grasshoppers release when they are captured. Chemical analysis of the liquid from the large grasshoppers known as desert locusts reveals a high terpene concentration, molecules acquired from their diet of toxin-laden desert plants. Not only are they immune to the terpenes that plants synthesize in self-defense, but these grasshoppers can save and use them as molecules for their protection against predators. A grasshopper that feeds exclusively on members of the milkweed family (Asclepiadaceae) exploits the cardiac glycosides that characterize the milkweeds; its toxic secretion contains calactin and calotropin, both plant-derived secondary compounds. When these grasshoppers are reared on a diet containing no milkweeds, the toxic chemicals in their defense secretions disappear.

Chrysomelid beetles that feed on willows (*Salix orestera* and *S. lasiolepis*) use the glycoside salicin from the trees to synthesize salicylaldehyde, the active ingredient in their defense secretion. Salicin was the active ingredient in willow infusions used in European folk medicine for the pain of headaches and gout. Naturally occurring salicin is a molecular starting point for the synthesis of salicylic acid, the chemical precursor of acetylsalicylic acid or aspirin. The rare, toxic amino acid L-canavanine occurs in the seed proteins of several legumes, where it serves as a potent growth inhibitor for herbivores, including mammals. The bruchid beetles that feed on the seeds of *Dioclea megacarpa,* a Costa Rican leguminous vine, have another strategy for using plant-made poisons. Although about 13 percent of a seed's dry weight is L-canavanine, a large dose of toxin for herbivores, the bruchid beetles have evolved biochemical

Figure 5-3. Glycosides from the common milkweed (*Asclepias syriaca*) are concentrated in the bodies of monarch butterfly larvae that feed on the leaves of various milkweeds.

pathways that allow them to use L-canavanine to synthesize amino acids for their proteins. This toxic amino acid is converted to urea, then ammonia, and eventually is used to supply the nitrogen-containing amino groups that occur in all amino acids, the molecules that link to form proteins.

The best-studied example of insects that use borrowed plant molecules for their defense is based on the chemistry of milkweeds (*Asclepias* spp.). Female monarch butterflies select milkweeds for egg-laying, and their larvae graze on milkweed leaves (Plate 7). The leaf tissues serve as a food and as a source of the cardiac glycosides that make the mature monarchs unpalatable to insect-eating birds. The larvae accumulate the glycosides, which eventually are concentrated in the wings of mature monarchs. The adults are brightly patterned, with distinctive black, white, and orange banding that marks their wings. This banding seems to be the functional opposite of camouflage and is a biological phenomenon known as warning coloration. Blue jays show gastric upset and vomiting when they ingest monarchs and soon learn to recognize and avoid the memorable banded pattern of the butterfly wings.

Many other examples are known of poisonous animals that have evolved distinct colors and patterns. Among these are vertebrates such as poisonous coral snakes, skunks, and unpalatable salamanders that advertise their hazards to potential predators. Several other milkweed-feeding insects such as the bright red cerambycid beetles and the bright green chrysomelid beetles also have warning coloration. Predators soon learn to avoid unpalatable prey, but they are easily deceived by a few nontoxic species such as the viceroy butterflies that mimic the warning coloration of monarchs. Viceroys lack the cardiac glycosides that render monarchs unpalatable and so are quite edible, but they avoid predation by sporting the orange and black bands reminiscent of the warning coloration of monarchs. In effect, they exploit the relationship between insect-eating birds and monarchs, but viceroys can be successful only if the adults appear late in the season, after the birds have learned to avoid eating the glycoside-laden monarchs. Then viceroys can masquerade as monarchs and avoid predation from birds that have already sampled monarchs. This strategy is known as Batesian mimicry, named for H. W. Bates, a nineteenth-century naturalist who traveled with Alfred Russel Wallace.

Swallowtail butterflies concentrate the furocoumarin molecules made by plants in the parsley family (Umbelliferae) such as Queen Anne's lace (*Daucus carota*) and celery (*Apium cepa*). These molecules include the psoralens, furocoumarin compounds that are toxic in the presence of light. In nature, psoralens not only protect plants from insect attack by rendering their predators photosensitive but also function as phytoalexins that prevent fungal infections. Phytoalexins are natural antibiotics that protect plants from invasion by pathogenic fungi. Leaf damage may stimulate the synthesis of psoralens; an insect grazing on celery leaves may find itself dosed with higher psoralen concentrations as leaves are damaged. In daylight, the ingested psoralens cross-link DNA, cause mutations, and interfere with normal cell division, but swallowtail caterpillars seem to be relatively immune to these effects. In their case the psoralens presumably are passed along to their predators, in the same way that

monarchs concentrate cardiac glycosides when they feed on milkweeds as larvae. The large black swallowtail butterflies exhibit warning coloration, and studies in Europe show that birds reject them as prey. In medicine, psoralens are used along with ultraviolet radiation to treat psoriasis,

Figure 5-4. The memorable warning coloration of the swallowtail butterfly is associated with the toxicity that the larvae acquire as they feed on Queen Anne's lace (*Daucus carota*) and other members of the parsley family (Umbelliferae).

although the potential for genetic damage to human tissue when psoralens are ingested is not fully known.

Chemical Evolution

Most known secondary compounds originate from the many diverse families of flowering plants, also known as angiosperms, and thousands more await discovery and analysis. They are among those molecules that historically constitute most of our pharmacopoeia, and they also provide much of our hope for future cures for diseases like cancer and AIDS. Teleology tempts us to imagine that these compounds evolved as medicines rather than as armaments in the frontline of plant defense, but in reality their existence and molecular diversity stem from the struggle for survival on earth.

As plants grow, they remain rooted firmly in place, stationary meals for browsing herbivores. Angiosperms have been able to respond to this problem with diverse, unique molecular defenses; the success of large families such as the daisies (Compositae) and umbellifers (Umbelliferae) suggests the efficiency of this strategy. Some paleontologists have suggested that angiosperms lived and diversified during the early years of their existence during the Cretaceous period because they were able to survive the attentions of hungry, plant-eating dinosaurs. Ferns and cycads, the botanical contemporaries of dinosaurs, synthesized high concentrations of tannins, while flowering plants evolved a range of additional secondary compounds. Distasteful and toxic compounds may have discouraged many large herbivores, and the high intrinsic growth rate of flowering plants may have helped them to recover quickly from intensive grazing. Natural phenomena such as chemical communication among plants and the coevolutionary "borrowing" of secondary compounds by insects are predictable outcomes of the widespread evolution of chemical defenses in flowering plants.

Angiosperms progressed from an early evolutionary "experiment" with flowers and fruit to their present status as the dominant plants on earth in part because of their abundant secondary compounds. These protective molecules reveal the potential for adaptation and the extent of the genetic diversity found in flowering plants, and they have served as an effective shield against herbivores as flowering plants have evolved to occupy almost every botanical niche. As potential human medicines, the diverse secondary compounds that contributed to angiosperm survival long before the start of human evolution may now secure our future as well.

CHAPTER 6

Significant Discoveries

O UR MEDICAL past has relied on healing plants. From times of prehistory, humans have used plants to cure infectious disease, treat debilitating conditions, ease the pain of childbirth and injury, and relieve melancholia and mental illness. East and West have had their traditions of medicinal botany, which now begin to meld into a global knowledge of botanical solutions to human problems. A midwestern student could use ginseng capsules to alleviate the symptoms of stress, while a headache-addled businessperson half a world away might reach for an aspirin tablet rather than a Chinese herb. Eventually, rain forest plants will integrate into worldwide awareness and use, and it will not be uncommon to reach into the medicine chest for a cure once known only to shamans. Future options are limited only by the extent of botanical biodiversity and our capacity for exploration. Our ancestors began this process for us and discovered many medicinal species that became significant to human health and well-being; this chapter is devoted to several of the many wild plants that have yielded important medicines in our pharmacopoeia.

Opium Poppy

The white poppy *Papaver somniferum* yields opium, an alkaloid mixture that is the earliest known painkiller, but this is plant chemistry that achieves extremes. Through history opium has alleviated more suffering than any other plant medicine, but it has also been the source of addiction, agony, and premature death. Native to Turkey and Asia Minor, these poppy plants have escaped cultivation and naturalized into the landscape in Europe, North Africa, Asia, and Mexico. Perhaps after years of domestication no truly wild opium poppies now exist; escaped plants invariably occur in agricultural fields and other disturbed sites near human activity. They are cultivated as a source of opium in India, China, Myanmar (formerly Burma), Vietnam, Indonesia, Turkey, the Balkans, and the Mediterranean region. A small portion of the current opium crop (possibly 5 percent) is used for pharmaceutical medicines; most opium is destined for the illegal drug trade, but the nonmedicinal, recreational use of opium is nothing new. Archeological evidence from Europe suggests that opium poppies were grown as a medicinal and psychoactive drug during the Neolithic and Bronze Ages.

Members of the poppy family (Papaveraceae) are characterized by alkaloid-laden latex, an opaque sap present throughout the plants. Opium, the dried latex of the immature poppy capsule, contains a mixture of twenty-six alkaloids, including morphine, codeine, laudanine, thebaine, and papaver-

Figure 6-1. The flowers of opium poppy (*Papaver somniferum*) mature into capsules that produce copious latex, the source of medicinal alkaloids such as morphine, codeine, and papaverine.

ine. The Ebers papyrus of ancient Egypt suggested the use of opium to quiet infants, and the Greeks boiled the entire plant to make a sleeping potion known as *meconium*. They also used opium, which they called *opos* (sap), and knew that the potent alkaloid mixture should be gathered from the immature capsule. Even today opium is harvested manually, following a process first described by Dioscorides during the first century. The capsule is cut crosswise and the latex is scraped from the wound, collected in a container, and eventually dried.

By the fifth century B.C. the addictive nature of opium was understood, and Hippocrates discouraged its use. During the second century A.D., the Greek physician Galen (ca. 130–200) recommended the use of opium for pain relief from a variety of ailments such as toothaches, but he also noted that it be used with caution. It became known as a dangerous drug that could induce death through a sleeplike state, and history is punctuated with examples of its use. Agrippina, second wife of the Emperor Claudius, used opium mixed in wine to poison her stepson, clearing the way to the throne for her son. Napoleon may have used it to euthanize sick and wounded troops during his campaign into Egypt and Asia. Nevertheless, opium became known as a drug that could be used as a substitute for alcohol. The spread of opium across Arab lands may be attributed to the spread of the Moslem faith; the Koran forbade wine, and followers of the prophet Mohammed destroyed vineyards during their travels, but the Koran mentioned nothing about drugs such as opium and hashish.

The Chinese surgeon Hua T'o (ca. 190–265) used an anesthetic of wine and opium, and a millennium later the medical school at Salerno, Italy, taught new physicians to use a potent mixture of opium, mandrake, henbane, poison hemlock, ivy, and mulberry juice during surgeries. In the fourteenth century Paracelsus abhorred compound drugs, believing that the effects of many plants would render the mixture ineffective; he was the first to prepare laudanum or tincture of opium, made by combining opium with pure alcohol. Apothecary shops in sixteenth-century England offered opium as a panacea for all brain ailments, and English physicians considered opium essential for the practice of medicine. During the nineteenth century, opium-based patent medicines became common. Preparations such as Godfrey's Cordial, Dr. Bateman's Pectoral Drops, Mrs. Winslow's Soothing Syrup, and Pierce's Golden Discovery were easily available, and adults and children alike unwittingly became opium addicts. Paregoric was another popular mixture that included licorice, camphor, and anise along with the opium; the name is derived from the Greek word *paregorikos,* which means "soothing," and until recently it was a familiar home remedy for teething children.

The connection between the literary world and opium addiction is particularly well documented. The effects of rheumatic fever led Samuel Taylor Coleridge to Kendal's Black Drop, a mixture of opium and camphor, and he progressed to laudanum and complete addiction; his poem "Kubla Khan" was inspired by his opium-induced state. Ironically, Thomas de Quincy's *Confessions of an English Opium-Eater* (1820) may have led many curious humans to experience opium and the likelihood of addiction.

In China opium poppies were first grown in gardens as decorative and medicinal plants, but by the eighteenth century opium smoking had become a serious problem. The British East India Company supplied Indian-grown opium to Chinese addicts, but during the 1830s the Chinese government banned opium imports. The first and second opium wars were fought over the rights of the British to engage in the lucrative import of opium into China; the British acquired the island of Hong Kong through the treaty that ended the first opium war in 1842.

Morphine functions specifically as an analgesic to deaden the sensations of pain, but it is also considered a soporific since it induces sleep. Opium also yields codeine, used medicinally to suppress coughing, and papaverine, which relaxes muscle tissues. Heroin is a semisynthetic version of morphine made from the original alkaloid structure; two $-CH_3$ groups are added to each natural morphine molecule. It was first developed at the German Bayer Works and was advertised ironically as a safe, nonaddictive painkiller, but it is now a banned because of its highly addictive nature. The Scottish physician Alexander Wood invented the hypodermic needle in 1853, in time for it to be used in the United States to administer morphine during the Civil War; morphine addiction became so widespread among men recuperating from wounds that it became known as the "soldiers' disease."

The opium alkaloids presumably are produced by the poppies as chemical defense from attack by herbivores. The molecules are concentrated in the developing fruit, where they probably serve as chemical protection for the seeds that contain the next generation. Its natural function aside, morphine in particular has also affected human lives, from causing addiction to alleviating pain. The addictive nature of morphine is a significant problem that might be eliminated with slight changes to its molecular structure. Pharmaceutical chemists working with the structure of opium alkaloids may eventually synthesize a nonaddicting drug based on the molecular "blueprints" that first evolved in a Eurasian poppy.

Coca

Like opium poppies, coca (*Erythroxylon coca*) yields a pain-relieving alkaloid with addictive qualities. Cocaine, a tropane alkaloid that structurally resembles the alkaloids produced by belladonna and henbane, induces euphoria and can be used as a local anesthetic. Coca trees and shrubs should not be confused with cacao (*Theobroma cacao*), the Mexican tree that is the source of chocolate; coca trees are native to the Andes of Peru and Bolivia, where they grow on the eastern slopes, and they are cultivated throughout Asia and South America. Cocaine occurs at low concentrations in the leaves, and the tradition of chewing coca leaves has Pre-Columbian origins. The bulging cheeks of a ceramic figure from Peru suggest that Indians chewed coca leaves as early as 1600 B.C.

The Incas referred to coca as the "divine plant," and local people used it to promote endurance, relieve fatigue, and overcome the effects of hunger and thirst while climbing and laboring in the steep Andean slopes. Originally coca was considered the property of Incan royalty, and the leaves were buried in their graves. When the Spanish learned of its special properties, they encouraged the use of coca by Indian workers to enhance their productivity. Following the local custom, dried leaves are dipped into powdered lime, formed into a ball, and placed into the mouth for chewing, where the alkaline lime enhances the effects of the coca alkaloids. Coca defines Indian life in the Andes, and trips in the mountains are measured in *cocadas,* the time that a coca quid retains it potency. The pioneering ethnobotanist Richard Evans Schultes used coca leaves while working among Andean Indians; the low cocaine concentration in intact coca leaves is not addictive and cannot be equated with the dangerous abuse of purified cocaine. Schultes wrote, "I naturally learned to chew toasted coca leaves and, finding it to be a most helpful custom when one must work hard and there is little food, I used coca for eight years while in these remote areas, with absolutely no desire to continue upon my return." It is debatable whether coca leaves used this way are truly medicinal, but they do promote survival under the cold, harsh conditions of the *altiplanos* at high altitudes of 12,000 to 13,000 feet.

European awareness of coca began with the South American plant collections made by Joseph de Jussieu (1704–1779), a Swiss physician and botanist. In 1860 the alkaloid cocaine was isolated from coca, and during the nineteenth century its use was promoted as an antidote to morphine addiction. Sherlock Holmes, a fictional character developed by Sir Arthur Conan Doyle, exhibited the symptoms of cocaine addiction, but eventually overcame the drug, describing the hypodermic needle as "an instrument of evil." Dr. Angelo Mariani prepared and marketed coca-based wine, elixir, tea, lozenges, and pastilles, products with a reputation for curing conditions ranging from poor voice in opera singers to seasickness, debilitation, and diabetes. Early coca-based medicines contained 2 to 4 percent cocaine, and like opium-based patent medicines they caused many inadvertent addictions. Advertised as a brain and nerve tonic at the time of its development in 1885, Coca-Cola contained cocaine until 1904, when the manufacturer removed it at government urging. Today the beverage is flavored with coca leaves that have been processed to remove alkaloids. The cola portion is derived from the seeds of *Cola acuminata,* a tropical African tree that produces the stimulating alkaloids caffeine and theobromine.

The use of cocaine as an anesthetic began with the observation that it causes localized numbness; it was used extensively in eye surgery and dentistry until safer alternatives were developed. Synthetic drugs such as procaine (trade name Novocain) are based in part on the molecular structure of cocaine. This example illustrates another way that plants contribute to the development of new medicines, by providing an effective molecular framework that can be used entirely or in part as a model for synthetic drugs.

Curare Plants

Need begets invention, and faced with the challenges of hunting in the jungle, South American Indians developed darts and arrows that could be tipped with deadly poisons. Among these are curare poisons, potent alkaloid mixtures that cause muscle paralysis in their prey. Curare mixtures vary by region and tribe and may contain extracts from thirty plants. Several species of the woody moonseed vine (*Chondrodendron*) in the moonseed family (Menispermaceae) produce high concentrations of tubocurarine; eight species are native to Peru and Brazil, and some have also been used medicinally as diuretics and tonics. In Brazil, the strength of a curare mixture is gauged by its effect on prey. A "one-tree curare" means that a monkey can reach just one more tree after being hit with a treated dart, while a less potent "three-tree curare" would allow the monkey to travel a bit further before paralysis dropped it from the canopy. The poisons are known locally as *woorai* and *urari,* which roughly translated mean "he, to whom it comes, falls."

Additional alkaloids such as strychnine and brucine are found in *Strychnos* species in the logania family (Loganiaceae), trees and woody vines that are used in curare preparation in the Old and New World tropics. Some may also be used medicinally despite their toxicity; weak doses of the alkaloids from the bark of *S. malaccensis* native to Indochina are used as a nerve tonic, while more concentrated solutions are used as curares for hunting. The seeds of *S. nux-vomica*, a species native to India, the East Indies, and Sri Lanka, have been the commercial source of strychnine, and the trees were also used in Southeast Asia for making arrow and dart poisons.

This example illustrates the valuable lesson that dose alone can distinguish medicine from poison. During the nineteenth century the medicine *nux vomica* was used to induce vomiting and treat human ailments ranging from epilepsy to impotence, but in larger amounts it was used to poison animals. *Nux vomica* extracts were also used to stimulate circulation and respiration, but that application was soon abandoned because the effective dose was almost equivalent to the toxic dose. Strychnine is now used occasionally to stimulate respiration if certain types of poisoning occur, but the most significant medical uses of curare plants originate instead with tubocurarine from moonseed vines.

Medical knowledge of tubocurarine began with the experiments of Charles Waterton in England. After collecting curare in 1812, he injected it into animals and realized that it killed them by relaxing the muscles involved in respiration. He commented that *woorai* poison "destroys life's action so gently, that the victim appears to be in no pain whatever; and probably, were the truth known, it feels none, save the momentary smart at the time the arrow enters." The French physiologist Claude Bernard experimented with the nerves and muscles of frogs and by 1850 realized that curare interferes with the junction between nerves and the muscles that they stimulate. Modern studies suggest that he was correct; tubocurarine seems to interfere with the binding sites of acetylcholine, the molecules that are released by nerve endings and stimulate muscle activity.

Early studies were done with nonstandardized curare, and its potency varied depending on the sample used. It was used to treat muscle paralysis in cases of lockjaw and to ease the last stages of rabies, but the actual plants and chemistry of various curare mixtures were unknown until relatively recently. The English physician Dr. Harold King isolated tubocurarine in 1935 from a dried specimen, probably *Chondrodendron tomentosum,* and this alkaloid became known as the chemical basis of modern medicinal applications of curare. Early clinical trials involved patients afflicted with spastic paralysis, and later medical uses included tubocurarine treatment for Parkinson's disease, St. Vitus's dance, and multiple sclerosis. It soon became a valued surgical adjunct that could be used to relax contracted muscles in eye, throat, and abdominal surgeries. Tubocurarine enhanced the effects of anesthesia so that lower amounts could be used, and surgery became safer. In a pattern that we have seen before, synthetic drugs such as pancuronium and vecuronium that are based on the same molecular structure now commonly replace the naturally occurring alkaloid tubocurarine.

Willows

Americans consume about 80 million aspirin tablets each year, but few realize that this is a medicine originally derived from willow trees (*Salix* spp.). Willow extracts were used in ancient Greece to treat pain and gout, and the Chickasaw Indians prepared root infusions of *Salix alba* to relieve headaches. In Europe willow infusions were used for centuries as a folk remedy for the fever and aches associated with many common illnesses. In 1763, Rev. Edmund Stone wrote to the president of the Royal Society, "There is a bark of an English tree, which I have found by experience to be a powerful astringent, and very efficacious in curing aguish and intermitting disorders." Stone creatively extrapolated from the traditional Doctrine of Signatures; since feverish illnesses were common in the cool, moist English countryside, he believed that the medicinal willows grew there to provide cures. He contended that "many natural maladies carry their cures along with them, or their remedies lie not far from their causes."

Willow extracts owe their astringent quality to the presence of the glycoside salicin, a compound that was first isolated during the nineteenth century from willows and poplars (*Populus* spp.). When ingested, salicin breaks down into salicylic acid and a simple sugar. Other plants have a similar chemistry; salicylic acid and the related compound methyl salicylate were found in a Eurasian meadowsweet (*Spiraea ulmaria,* now *Filipendula ulmaria*), wintergreen (*Gaultheria procumbens*), and black birch (*Betula lenta*). Methyl salicylate is known as oil of wintergreen, a familiar flavoring and a traditional cure for "aguish disorders" or fevers. Both salicin and methyl salicylate were used to treat painful conditions such as arthritis and to relieve fevers, but salicylic acid can cause stomach pain, bleeding, and nausea. Nevertheless, salicylic acid became a common, inexpensive treatment for the symptoms of rheumatic fever, gout, and arthritis. It was first synthesized in the laboratory in 1875.

Aspirin, the most common salicylate compound, was first developed to treat the arthritis that plagued the father of a German chemist. Felix Hoffman worked in the Bayer division of I. G. Farben, a German company that produced aniline dye, and his elderly father suffered from rheumatoid arthritis. The elder Hoffman found that salicylic acid caused acute stomach pain, but his son searched the literature and in 1893 discov-

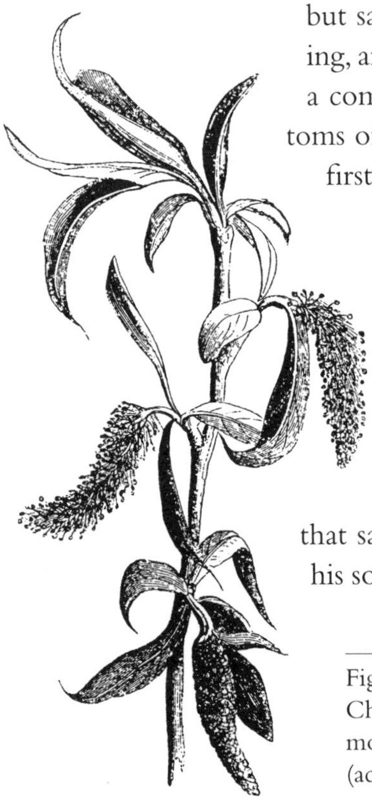

Figure 6-2. White willow (*Salix alba*) was used by the Chickasaw Indians to treat headaches, foreshadowing modern use of the related semi-synthetic drug aspirin (acetylsalicylic acid) for similar ailments.

ered acetylsalicylic acid, a less acidic alternative. This milder form was named "aspirin," taking the "a" from "acetyl" and "spirin" from "*Spiraea,*" and it soon became a universal drug for pain, fever, and inflammation. It was first sold in 1899 as a powder, and aspirin tablets were marketed in 1915. As part of the Treaty of Versailles at the end of World War I, Germany surrendered the brand name Aspirin to the United States, England, France, and Russia. Judge Learned Hand later ruled that no individual pharmaceutical company owned the name aspirin or could demand royalties for its use; aspirin became the universally known name for acetylsalicylic acid.

Aspirin is now the mostly widely used drug in the Western pharmacopoeia, although it has only about one-tenth the potency of morphine for relieving pain. While aspirin has traditionally been used to treat fever, pain, and inflammation, it also interferes with blood clotting and thus can prevent strokes and heart attacks in calibrated doses. As an anticoagulant, it prevents aggregates of blood platelets that can interfere with blood supply to the brain or heart, a serendipitous side effect that eventually will be more significant than its use as an analgesic.

Snakeroot

Snakeroot (*Rauvolfia serpentina*) is a small shrub native to India, Sri Lanka, and the East Indies that was used locally for mental illness and snakebite, long before it was "discovered" by Western medicine. More than three thousand years ago, the Indian *Rig Veda* mentioned snakeroot in its verses that describe medicinal plants. In Hindi it is known as *chandra* or "moon," a reference to its use for "moon disease" or lunacy, and it is also sold as *pagal-ke-dawa,* the traditional herb for insanity. Indian peasants and medicine men and women knew snakeroot, named because the twisted, woody roots suggest the form of a snake; this seems to be a coincidental example of the Doctrine of Signatures in which the plant is a true cure for the ailment. Reserpine, the major medicinal alkaloid in snakeroot, lowers blood pressure and is considered an effective antidote to the bites of poisonous snakes and scorpions. Snakeroot was also used to calm crying babies, and Mahatma Gandhi sipped tea steeped from the leaves when he wanted to experience a state of calm detachment.

The Dutch physician and botanist G. E. Rumpf (1627–1702) related a tale of mongoose behavior, probably fanciful, in which the animal eats snakeroot leaves to protect itself from the bite of a venomous snake. He attributed human knowledge of snakeroot to observations of mongoose behavior, "Men seem to have learned the powers of this plant from the so-called mongoose or weasel. This little animal, before attacking a snake, fortifies itself by eating the leaves. . . . It is said to cure the bite of most poisonous snakes, even the *Cobra capella.*" More likely, snakeroot became known medicinally because its obvious serpentine roots could be used successfully to treat the symptoms of venomous snakebites.

Snakeroot shrubs are cultivated for medicinal use in tropical India, and the roots are dried and ground into a powder that contains fifty alkaloids. This chemistry is typical of the dogbane family (Apocynaceae), which includes the Madagascar periwinkle (*Catharanthus roseus*) used in cancer treatment. By the beginning of the twentieth century, snakeroot was cultivated as a curiosity in the botanic gardens at Bogor in Java, but its modern use began during the 1920s with a review of ancient medicinal Indian plants. Research was hampered by lack of funding and distrust of Hindu Ayurvedic medicinal practices, but in 1931 two chemists in New Delhi isolated several crystalline substances (probably alkaloid mixtures) from snakeroot. These substances were used for clinical trials in India, where snakeroot proved effective as a sedative in cases of mental illness and acute insomnia, and it also lowered blood pressure.

Initially there was very little interest in snakeroot outside India, but E. R. Squibb and Sons eventually obtained some tablets for testing. Snakeroot soon became a well-regarded drug in Western medicine for high blood pressure and mental illness; it reduced the need for electric shock treatment, ended drastic surgery such as lobotomy, and was hailed as the most significant advance in psychiatric medicine. Reserpine, among the potent snakeroot alkaloids, was first isolated in 1952, and this allowed standardized doses to be administered. A few years later, reserpine was synthesized in the laboratory by Dr. Robert Woodward of Harvard University. By 1957, more than fifteen hundred papers on the medical uses of snakeroot had been published, ranging from the treatment of schizophrenia and paranoia to easing the misery of withdrawal in cases of drug addiction. Most importantly, the success of this medicinal plant demonstrated that psychiatric disorders were physiological abnormalities that could be treated chemically, with either natural or synthetic drugs.

In 1954, concerned that snakeroot might be exterminated by overcollection, Indian government officials imposed a brief embargo on its export. Soon several drug companies initiated plans to cultivate the plants. Exploration in Africa revealed that the related species *Rauvolfia vomitoria* had high concentrations of reserpine, and it is now the major commercial source of the alkaloid. The ethnobotany of *R. vomitoria* in western Africa includes its use by local peoples as a sedative, foreshadowing its use in Western medicine. A third species (*R. canescens*) was introduced from the Caribbean into India and is the source of deserpidine, which is also used to treat high blood pressure.

The snakeroot alkaloids work slowly over a few weeks to reduce blood pressure by blocking the neurotransmitter molecules (norepinephrine) that transmit nerve signals between the sympathetic nervous system and the heart and blood vessels. Blocking the neurotransmitter molecules relaxes blood vessels and heart output, and blood pressure decreases. In severe cases, snakeroot is used along with alkaloids from false hellebore (*Veratrum viride*), a member of the lily family (Liliaceae) that was used by Native American tribes to treat high blood pressure. The use of reserpine to treat mental illness has now been eclipsed by synthetic drugs, but its discovery by Western physicians remains an important milestone in the history of medicine.

Kombe

Curare poisons are complex, variable botanical mixtures, and in Africa one ingredient may be the macerated seeds of *kombe,* a vine (*Strophanthus kombe*) that is another member of the important medicinal family Apocynaceae. During the nineteenth century, the explorer and missionary Dr. David Livingstone predicted its medicinal use, "We observed natives hunting with poisoned arrows. The poison is called '*kombe*'. . . . It is very virulent, but *kombe* may turn out to be a valuable remedy." His companion, Sir John Kirk, collected the fruit and brought the specimens back to England, where they were described and identified at the Royal Botanic Gardens. A trace of *kombe* juice contacted the toothbrush which Kirk carried in his pocket; he noted its bitter taste and its effect that seemed to decrease his pulse, which sparked interest in the physiological action of the compounds in *Strophanthus.* Oral doses can cause cardiac arrest and respiratory failure, and although some African tribes considered *Strophanthus* a panacea, its dangers were understood. When *kombe* is used as an arrow poison in hunting animals for food, tannin-rich tree sap from baobab (*Adansonia digitata*) is used to neutralize the effects of any toxin remaining in the meat.

The cardiac glycoside strophanthin was isolated from *Strophanthus kombe* in 1885, and it became a popular cardiotonic drug in many countries despite its potential hazards. Ouabain, also known as G-strophanthin, is a related cardiac drug that is isolated from the seeds of *S. gratus.* The molecular structure of both is similar to the cardiac glycosides produced by foxglove and consists of a steroid molecule bonded to a sugar. The steroid sarmentogenin found in *Strophanthus* seeds sparked interest because its molecular structure could provide a molecular starting point for the synthesis of cortisone, if sufficient quantities of *Strophanthus* seeds could be obtained.

Until this time, the cortisone needed to treat rheumatoid arthritis and rheumatic fever was obtained from animal sources. Cortisone was prohibitively expensive because its laboratory synthesis from bile acids was a complex procedure consisting of several individual reactions. A chemical shortcut to cortisone production using a botanical compound would be a medical major advance, but botanical expeditions to Africa during 1949 failed to locate sufficient quantities of seed from wild plants of *Strophanthus* species to provide the crude extracts needed for cortisone synthesis. A typical square mile of African forest supports only about ten *Strophanthus* vines, and harvesting must be done just when the fruits are ripe.

Early experiments with cultivation were similarly discouraging. The forest pollinators did not visit the field-grown vines, and seed production proved unreliable. There was a further complication; in their natural habitats, the vines grew up trees, but in fields they required 100-foot supports that were expensive and impractical to build. During the 1950s, tropical yams (*Dioscorea* spp.) became a more practical source of precursors for cortisone and oral contraceptives; individual tubers weigh twenty to thirty pounds, and there are several yam species that produce steroids. *Strophanthus* species still remain relatively unknown and may yield future medicines; interesting ethnobotanical uses that merit investigation include the treatment of skin ulcerations, venereal disease, and parasites. Nevertheless, the practical lessons are well learned. In this case, wild plants proved insufficient as a source, and widespread cultivation of the vines seemed unlikely. Whenever large quantities of a botanical compound are required, there must be a reliable source; the future of a medicinal plant depends not only on its chemistry but also on aspects of its growth and ecology that define its potential as a natural resource.

Madagascar Periwinkle

During the mid-eighteenth century, botanists at the Jardin des Plantes in Paris sent seeds of the Madagascar periwinkle (*Catharanthus roseus,* formerly *Vinca rosea*) to the Chelsea Physic Garden in London. Philip Miller, curator at the Chelsea garden, cultivated *C. roseus* and sent its seeds worldwide, and in tropical areas the plants have frequently naturalized into the local roadside flora. In Puerto Rico and Cuba, the flowers are made into a decoction that is used as an eyewash, and in the West Indies and South Africa the Madagascar periwinkle was long used as a folk cure for diabetes. Eventually patent medicines such as Vinculin in England and Covinca in South Africa were marketed as treatments for diabetes. These claims may have some validity; experimental injections of a periwinkle extract have been effective in decreasing the symptoms in a group of diabetic adults. Additional folk uses abound; the roots are used as an abortifacient in the Philippines and to treat malaria in Vietnam, while in Chinese folk medicine a leaf and stem decoction is used for kidney complaints.

More than seventy alkaloids have been isolated from the Madagascar periwinkle, including two that have proven to be effective agents against leukemia and Hodgkin's disease, a cancer of the lymph nodes. Its use as a source of anticancer alkaloids arose from its reputation as a folk cure for diabetes, which resulted in preliminary laboratory investigations by the Eli Lily Company during the 1950s. Laboratory animals developed critically low counts of white blood cells, leaving them defenseless against infections caused by bacteria. This result suggested that one or more of the periwinkle alkaloids might slow or halt white blood cell production, and this is probably the mechanism that evolved in nature to discourage herbivorous predators from eating Madagascar periwinkles. Periwinkle extracts were effective against mouse

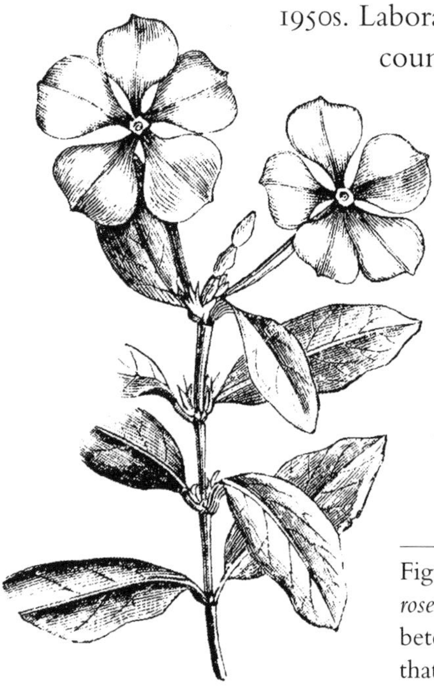

Figure 6-3. Madagascar periwinkle (*Catharanthus roseus*) was first used in patent medicines for diabetes and later found to be a source of alkaloids that could be used in cancer chemotherapy.

leukemia in 1957, and during the 1960s this resulted in new cancer chemotherapies derived from isolated periwinkle alkaloids. Vinblastine is used in cases of Hodgkin's disease and choriocarcinoma, while vincristine has proven effective for childhood leukemias and breast cancer.

Pacific Yew

The cool, moist forests of the Pacific Northwest are mixed old-growth ecosystems, the natural habitat of the spotted owl and the native yew tree that is the primary source of the anticancer drug paclitaxel, more commonly known by its trademark name of Taxol. (Taxol is both a generic name and a brand name.) The bark, leaves, and roots of Pacific yew (*Taxus brevifolia*) produce paclitaxel, a complex terpene-based molecule that may serve an adaptive function by inhibiting the growth of parasitic fungi that thrive in the damp forest soil. Yews, once considered small "trash" trees by the timber industry, were routinely burned after clear-cutting; perhaps 90 percent of the original yew population disappeared before its medicinal value was realized. The antitumor properties of paclitaxel were discovered only during a routine screening of North American plants in the 1960s at the National Cancer Institute. Extracts of the Pacific yew were found to stop the growth of several mouse tumors, a case in which ethnobotany provided no clues. Native Americans did not use the trees specifically for cancers or tumors, but an early ethnobotany reference noted that the Bella Coola tribe of British Columbia used Pacific yew for lung ailments, which may have foreshadowed the present. Paclitaxel is now used to treat lung cancers that do not respond to other therapies.

Cancers exhibit uncontrolled cell division, and paclitaxel stops malignant tumors from growing by interfering with the microtubules that are responsible for dividing the chromosomes during cell division. The microtubules do not disassemble after cell division is complete, and so many microtubules accumulate in the cytoplasm

that cell divisions cease. Paclitaxel inhibits the separation of the tubu-
lin molecules, the protein subunits that compose the microtubules,
providing a unique method of interfering with cancerous growth.
Clinical trials during the early 1980s revealed that paclitaxel could
help in 30 percent of the advanced cases of ovarian cancer, and the
drug shows promise for other malignancies as well.

Pacific yew research has explored several pathways, ranging from
the laboratory synthesis of paclitaxel to hunting for alternative *Taxus*
species that also yield paclitaxel from their bark and needles. There
were early successes with partial synthesis of paclitaxel, a complex
molecule consisting of several interconnected carbon rings. Robert
Holton of Florida State University produced partially synthetic paclitaxel starting with compounds from the needles of English yew (*T.
baccata*), a shrub commonly cultivated in hedges. The patented drug
Taxotere is based on the structure of docetaxel, with slight changes
to the side groups of atoms that are bonded to the carbon rings.
Because it is derived from the needles of English yew, it does not
require stripping bark from endangered Pacific yews. Research
groups have also produced synthetic paclitaxel, along with several
similar molecules that are known as analogs; some analogs may prove
more effective in antitumor activity than paclitaxel itself.

The cost of the synthetic drugs is high, and Pacific yew is a slow-
growing species. Cultivated trees need seventy to one hundred years
to grow a trunk four inches in diameter, the minimum size for harvesting. Wild resources are also sparse, since only about 10 percent of
the scattered wild trees are large enough to yield sufficient bark.
Another of the seven species of *Taxus* might prove to be a better
paclitaxel source; these range from a Philippine yew that grows to
ninety feet to a low, creeping Canadian shrub. One of the least
known is the Mexican yew (*Taxus globosa*), which Rob Nicholson
and four other botanists found during a 1990 expedition to the
Sierra Madre Oriental region of northeastern Mexico. Specimens
were collected from marked trees so that trees yielding high concentrations of paclitaxel as a result of natural variation could be identi-

fied, and later analysis showed that some trees produce ten times more paclitaxel than others. The medicinal demand for yews may also yield some coincidental benefits; Mexican yews are now being cultivated in Peru as a replacement crop for narcotic plants.

Perhaps the most surprising related discovery occurred a few years ago in Montana, when chemist Andrea Stierle found a parasitic fungus on yew bark that produces small amounts of paclitaxel even after removal from its host tree. Paclitaxel production continued in the fungus even after several generations were grown in the laboratory. The biological question is obvious: Why do a coniferous tree and fungus share the ability to produce the same complex molecule? Possibly the fungus acquired copies of the genes for producing paclitaxel from its host tree. Gene transfer from organism to organism does occasionally occur in nature, and paclitaxel may benefit the fungus by inhibiting the growth of competing microorganisms. Besides paclitaxel, the fungus produces some additional molecules that have the same characteristic carbon ring structure as paclitaxel.

Fungi grow quickly and are easily cultured in large batches; this fungus, now named *Taxomyces andreanae* after its discoverer, may prove to be a better source of paclitaxel (taxol) than either yew trees or laboratory synthesis. Altering the growth conditions of the fungus or changing the fungus genetically may eventually result in paclitaxel yields that are sufficient for commercial production. This situation would be ideal because paclitaxel could be produced inexpensively and in sufficient quantity for all patients, and the old–growth forests that are the original Pacific yew habitats could remain intact.

Medicinal Futures

Suffering has been alleviated and lives saved by the plants that we do know, and we can anticipate the future of medicinal botany by contemplating the successes of the past. Our present knowledge of plant medicines represents a small portion of the natural resources that still await discovery because relatively few secondary compounds have been characterized and examined for their medicinal potential. Perhaps most exciting will be cures for various cancers, botanical drugs with the potential to slow or stop malignant growth that will be analogous to the periwinkle alkaloids and paclitaxel in their value. Similarly, we should not overlook the medicinal potential of familiar herbal species that have been used for millennia. All these plants are only the preliminary chapters of medicinal botany, with many more to be written in future decades.

PLATE 1. Yarrow (*Achillea millefolium*) contains more than one hundred biologically active secondary compounds and has been used in Europe and in North America to treat colds, fevers, and bleeding wounds.

PLATE 2. According to the Doctrine of Signatures, the wiry black stems of maidenhair fern (*Adiantum pedatum*) recommended its use for hair problems, but during the nineteenth century it was recognized as an effective treatment for asthma and congestion.

PLATE 3. *Aesculus indica* (shown here) has close relatives in Europe and North America, including the European horsechestnut *A. hippocastanum,* which is also used to treat rheumatism.

PLATE 4. Kukui (*Aleurites moluccana*) is an oil-producing tree that early Polynesians carried and planted throughout the Pacific region, where they used it to treat thrush and other skin diseases.

PLATE 5. Horseradish (*Armoracia rusticana*) contains mustard oils, sulfur-containing glycosides that characterize the mustard poultices and plasters used to treat various ills.

PLATE 6. American colonists used root tea prepared from
swamp milkweed (*Asclepias incarnata*) as a heart tonic, but its
cardiac glycosides are potentially toxic. Courtesy New England Wild Flower Society.

PLATE 7. Monarch butterfly larvae feed on the leaves of milkweeds (*Asclepias* spp.) and acquire bitter cardiac glycosides that protect them from predators. Courtesy New England Wild Flower Society.

PLATE 8. Butterfly weed (*Asclepias tuberosa*) contains cardiac glycosides and was an ingredient in Lydia Pinkham's Vegetable Compound. Shakers used its roots to treat chest inflammations. Courtesy New England Wild Flower Society.

PLATE 9. Chimpanzees in the Mahale Mountains National Park of western Tanzania swallow the intact hairy leaves of *Aspilia mossambicensis,* which may help to dislodge internal parasites from intestinal walls. Photo by Michael A. Huffman.

PLATE 10. During the rainy season, when parasites are abundant, chimpanzees swallow between fifteen and thirty-five leaves of *Aspilia mossambicensis* at a sitting. Photo by Michael A. Huffman.

PLATE 11. Marijuana (*Cannabis sativa*) has been used medicinally to treat the symptoms of glaucoma and the nausea associated with chemotherapy. Courtesy New England Wild Flower Society.

PLATE 12. Celandine poppy (*Chelidonium majus*) releases yellow latex, which suggested the plant's early use for jaundice, but the species was also used to treat skin afflictions such as eczema and ringworm.

PLATE 13. Black cohosh (*Cimicifuga racemosa*) promotes the synthesis of estrogen in females and traditionally has been used for reproductive ailments in women.

PLATE 14. Taro (*Colocasia antiquorum*) was carried by canoe to many Polynesian islands, where it was grown as a staple starchy crop and a medicinal plant that could be used to treat wounds, infections, and insect stings.

PLATE 15. Yellow lady's slipper (*Cypripedium calceolus* var. *pubescens*) was used to treat depression and despondency, and its popularity caused the disappearance of most wild populations.

PLATE 16. The popularity of herbal medicines containing purple coneflower (*Echinacea purpurea*) and related species has jeopardized wild coneflower populations. Courtesy New England Wild Flower Society.

PLATE 17. Mayflower or gravel plant (*Epigaea repens*) was grown and marketed by nineteenth-century Shakers as an effective cure for kidney stones.

PLATE 18. Ground ivy (*Glechoma hederacea*) was introduced from Europe as a medicinal herb to treat kidney ailments, wounds, and lunacy, but now it is naturalized in American lawns and meadows.

PLATE 19. Goldenseal (*Hydrastis canadensis*) is gradually disappearing from northern forests, the result of overcollection as a medicinal herb since the end of the nineteenth century. Courtesy New England Wild Flower Society.

PLATE 26. Despite its traditional use as a healing herb, comfrey (*Symphytum officinale*) is a potentially toxic species that contains liver-damaging pyrrolizidine alkaloids in its roots.

PLATE 27. Its essential oils are now recognized as potentially lethal, but tansy (*Tanacetum vulgare*) was introduced from Europe by colonists who used it to brew a weak tea to treat dyspepsia and digestive ailments.

PLATE 24. Bloodroot (*Sanguinaria canadensis*) synthesizes the antibacterial alkaloid sanguinarine that is included in toothpaste to slow the growth of oral bacteria, perhaps foreshadowed by the earlier use of bloodroot in cough syrups and to treat laryngitis. Courtesy New England Wild Flower Society.

PLATE 25. Steroid-containing glycoalkaloids from woody nightshade (*Solanum dulcamara*) are used as a starting point for the laboratory synthesis of medicinal steroids.

PLATE 22. Ginseng (*Panax quinquefolius*) has been collected for export to Asia before 1720, and its commercial trade is regulated by international treaty. Courtesy New England Wild Flower Society.

PLATE 23. American colonists considered May apple (*Podophyllum peltatum*) the equivalent of the European mandrake, and more recently it has been used to make a semi-synthetic drug for treating testicular cancers. Courtesy New England Wild Flower Society.

PLATE 20. Controlled doses of dicoumarins derived from sweet clover (*Melilotus officinalis*) are used medicinally as anticoagulants to break apart blood clots. Courtesy New England Wild Flower Society.

PLATE 21. Bee balm or Oswego tea (*Monarda didyma*) is a native American species that contains thymol, an antiseptic, and was used as a tea substitute after the Boston Tea Party in 1773. Courtesy New England Wild Flower Society.

PLATE 28. Valerian (*Valeriana officinalis*) produces terpenes known as valepotriates that are common ingredients in herbal tranquilizers sold in Europe. Courtesy New England Wild Flower Society.

PLATE 29. When they are sick, chimpanzees in the Mahale Mountains National Park of western Tanzania chew the bitter pith of *Vernonia amygdalina,* which seems to control the growth of intestinal parasites. Photo by Michael A. Huffman

PLATE 30. An infusion made from the crushed leaves and twigs of *Vernonia amygdalina* is used in Africa to treat intestinal problems and parasites, and related plants in Asia and South America have similar ethnobotanical applications. Photo by Michael A. Huffman.

CHAPTER 7

~

Zoopharmacognosy and Botanical Toxins

PARASITES and plagues are nothing new, and animals and humans have suffered from illness from the time of their origins. Our earliest ancestors learned to identify and use specific plants to treat various ailments, and this knowledge constitutes the historical basis of modern medicinal botany. Archaeology yields pertinent evidence; sixty thousand years ago, Neanderthals prepared a gravesite inside a cave in the highlands of Iraq. The buried man was surrounded by eight plants, seven of them now recognized as medicinal plants. Among these was an *Ephedra* species, a small woody shrub with conelike reproductive parts that was most likely used medicinally rather than for decoration. The several *Ephedra* species native to Iraq are now used as cardiac stimulants and to treat asthma and bronchitis, and it is quite possible that Neanderthals used them in similar ways.

Practical knowledge of plants passed to the descendants of early hominids and eventually to humans, but another question merits consideration. Could other animals, particularly nonhuman primates, possibly acquire the knowledge and ability to use medicinal plants? Daniel Janzen, naturalist and tropical biologist, was the first to suggest in 1978 that the secondary compounds in some plants eaten by animals might help to control their internal parasites and micro-

Figure 7-1. African colobus monkeys may avoid internal parasites by including plants laden with secondary compounds in their diet.

bial disease. He related the absence of parasites in African black and red colobus monkeys with secondary compounds in their diets. He argued that if animals can learn to avoid toxic plants, they might also learn to eat plants that provide cures for ailments; the protection provided by certain plants in an animal's diet may be part of the balanced relationship between host animal and its parasites. It is unclear whether the use of medicinal plants is instinctive or learned behavior, but similar questions can be asked about many adaptive animal behaviors such as courtship rituals and nest-building strategies that enhance the chances of a species for reproduction and survival.

How can a plant that is part of an animal's diet be categorized definitely as food or medicine? The answers will come with the analysis of feeding behavior, plants consumed, and animal health. The behavior of wild chimpanzees and other animals suggests that this is a rich new area for cross-disciplinary research, an area of study that combines the disciplines of animal behavior, anthropology, and medicinal botany. The new term *zoopharmacognosy* was coined by Eloy Rodriguez and Richard Wrangham in their 1992 presentation "Zoopharmacognosy: Medicinal Plant Use by Wild Apes and Monkeys" to the American Association for the Advancement of Science. Pooled knowledge and research will reveal patterns in animal interactions with medicinal plants that may ultimately yield new sources of human medicines.

Chimpanzees and Self-Medication

Chimpanzees spend most of their waking hours searching for sustenance, and their diet consists of a varied mix of leaves, fruits, insects, and even meat. As a rule, food is chewed carefully and not swallowed intact, but a different eating strategy was described more than twenty years ago by Richard Wrangham, a Harvard anthropologist working in the Gombe National Park of Tanzania. He observed chimpanzees selecting the leaves of *Aspilia* species (Plate 9), folding and rubbing them against the inside of their mouths for a few seconds, and then gulping them intact. Often the leaves were gathered and swallowed early in the morning, possibly by animals afflicted with illness or parasites. This behavior is quite different from the usual pattern of leaf-eating, in which a handful

Figure 7-2. Chimpanzee behavior includes the swallowing of whole leaves of *Aspilia* spp. and the eating of the bitter pith of *Vernonia amygdalina* and *V. colorata,* both interpreted as examples of possible self-medication.

of leaves is swallowed after being thoroughly chewed. The un-chewed *Aspilia* leaves are often excreted intact in the chimpanzees' feces.

Aspilia mossambicensis (Plate 10) is a shrub in the daisy family (Compositae) with large leaves covered in dense hairs; it was assumed that secondary compounds produced by *Aspilia* had medicinal effects in the chimpanzees. Indeed, early reports from the lab of Eloy Rodriguez of Cornell University suggested that *Aspilia* leaves produce a red oil known as thiarubrine-A, which kills viruses, fungi, and parasitic worms, but this work has not been confirmed by other investigators. Chemistry aside, an alternative explanation for the swallowing of the intact *Aspilia* leaves is that their densely hairy surface may physically dislodge parasitic worms from the chimpanzees' intestines as ingested material moves through during digestion. The chimpanzees at Gombe swallow more *Aspilia* leaves during the rainy season, when there are more parasite larvae in their habitat and the likelihood of infection increases; they may consume between fifteen and thirty-five leaves at a sitting. African people in the same area use *Aspilia* to treat infections, malaria, and scurvy, as well as conditions such as sciatica and lumbago.

Chimpanzees swallow the leaves of several other African plants, including a native fig (*Ficus exasperata*) and species of *Commelina*. Leaves of *Ficus exasperata* contain a potent psoralen, a furocoumarin that kills nematode worms. At Mahale, an African site near Gombe, a male chimpanzee with a severe intestinal nematode infection was observed to consume many *Ficus* leaves over several days, with a reduction in his parasite load and improvement in his health. The Mahale chimpanzees also use leaves of *Commelina*, which are gathered and swallowed in the early morning hours. Coincidentally, the Shuar Indians of Amazonian Ecuador prepare a leaf tea of *Commelina* that is sipped before breakfast to treat headaches; perhaps the chimpanzees are deriving a similar effect from swallowing the *Commelina* leaves. Additional field studies are needed to learn whether such plants are being consumed exclusively for their medical value, or whether their medicinal effects are merely a benefit of their use as part of the chimpanzee diet.

Leaf-swallowing occurs in other animals as well. Pygmy chimpanzees (bonobos) in the Democratic Republic of the Congo (formerly Zaire) consume fern fronds, and eastern lowland gorillas also seek the leaves of *Commelina*. African great apes have been observed swallowing the intact leaves of thirty plant species from thirteen families; in some cases the animals are visibly ill, but in other cases they appear quite healthy. Several plants foraged by chimpanzees for possible medicinal uses are also used by local African people, including *Rubia cordifolia*, which is cultivated locally and used for various stomach ailments, and *Aneilema aequinoctiale*, which is used to treat fevers and earaches.

Leaves are not the only plant parts that animals may use medicinally. Chimpanzees chew the bitter pith from young shoots of two closely related species, *Vernonia amygdalina* (Plate 29) and *V. colorata*, woody composites with abundant secondary compounds that include sesquiterpene lactones and glycosides. The secondary compounds present in *Vernonia* leaves show antibiotic and antitumor activity, while also inhibiting the movement and reproduction of parasitic worms. The steroid-containing glycosides of *Vernonia* species interfere with the life cycles of the trematode worms that cause an affliction called schistosomiasis. *Vernonia* compounds also show activity against drug-resistant strains of *Plasmodium*, the single-celled blood parasite that causes malaria.

Michael Huffman, a primatologist at Kyoto University, believes that the secondary compounds of *Vernonia* species are toxic to the chimpanzees and that controlled doses of these bitter chemicals are consumed for their medicinal properties alone. Chimpanzees that are apparently ill consume small amounts of the bitter pith; otherwise, the plants are not part of their normal diet. Huffman was able to document the effectiveness of self-medication when parasite levels dropped dramatically in a chimpanzee twenty hours after she consumed *Vernonia* pith. A human parallel also occurs. *Vernonia* is known locally in Tanzania as *mujonso* or the "bitter leaf" tree; the leaves and twigs are crushed in cold water to treat the pain associated with intestinal parasites that plague humans as well as other primates. One species, *V. amygdalina* (Plate 30) has widespread use among the sub-Saharan peoples of Africa for intestinal problems and internal parasites, and related species of *Vernonia* have similar uses in Asia and South America. In Cameroon, leaves of *V. amygdalina* are used to prepare a bitter dish called *ndole,* which is eaten with meat and plantains and is said to restore stamina.

The feeding behavior of a chimpanzee is learned as the young animal associates with its mother and other elders. A young chimpanzee closely mimics the selection and preparation of foods, such as the removal of leaves and peeling away of bark to reveal the edible pith of a twig. Adult chimpanzees do not teach each other or urge peers to consume medicinal plants, but behavior such as leaf-swallowing and pith-eating could be acquired in youth. Possibly a few mature individuals experiment with plants that are not normally part of the chimpanzee diet, benefit from their medicinal effects, and pass this behavior along to their offspring and other younger members of their social group.

Gorilla Fruits

Gorillas feed voraciously on a range of edibles, from rotten wood to fruits, leaves, stems, and bark. They feed continuously, often just a few meters from yesterday's meal site. Working in Bwindi National Park in southwestern Uganda, John Berry of Cornell University has documented forty plants that provide food for the indigenous mountain gorillas, but the distinction between nutrition and medicine is not always clear. The brilliant red berries of a wild ginger, *Aframomum angustifolium,* one of the fruits selected and eaten by gorillas, are also sold in local marketplaces, and Ugandan children favor their sweet taste. The berries are used medicinally in Gabon, but Berry has commented that eating the fruit caused a burning sensation in his stomach, possibly indicating the effect of the water-soluble antibiotic on normal bacteria. In the laboratory, extracts of *Aframomum* fruit prevent the growth of bacteria, including strains of *Pseudomonas* and *Escherichia coli* (commonly known as *E. coli*).

Studies with gorillas in the field are a particular challenge; the population of mountain gorillas studied at Bwindi National Park has been reduced to about thirteen animals, but studies of *Aframomum* with captive lowland gorillas may reveal additional clues about the role of an antibiotic fruit in gorilla diets. The antimicrobial compounds in *Aframomum* may temporarily disrupt the beneficial bacteria in the digestive system of gorillas that graze on the fruits. On the other hand, each fruit eaten may serve as an antibiotic capsule that protects gorillas and humans against a range of tropical bacterial diseases. Perhaps the normal digestive bacteria of the gorillas are adapted to the presence of antibiotic compounds in the same way that some bacteria have selectively become resistant to the antibiotics used in human medicine.

New World Forests

The Atlantic forest of Brazil is the habitat of the largest New World monkeys, the muriquis or woolly spider monkeys, primates fully adapted to an arboreal life amidst incredible botanical diversity; these forests are reduced to 5 percent of their original range, and the muriquis are now an endangered species. The monkeys travel through the canopy in search of leaves, flowers, and fruit, and occasionally they descend to the ground where they feed on ferns, bamboo and other grasses, and tree bark. High energy foods, essentially a variety of flowers and fruits, are their preferred meals, although about half their feeding time is devoted to leaf grazing. By feeding on a range of plant parts, the muriquis are adapted to the Atlantic forest, which because of its distance from the equator has distinct periods of flowering.

Much of what is known about the muriquis and their feeding habits comes from field studies at Fazenda Montes Claros conducted by Karen Strier of the University of Wisconsin. She has tracked the

Figure 7-3. Muriquis or woolly spider monkeys ingest large quantities of secondary compounds in their diet, which may both affect their reproductive cycles and control internal parasites.

muriquis, observed their food selection habits, and collected fecal samples for parasite analysis in the laboratory. Muriquis digest food rapidly and defecate several times each day, suggesting that any toxic secondary compounds from their plant diet pass rapidly from their systems. They are an active species, fully at home in the canopy, and require an energy-rich diet that includes the floral products of pollen and nectar. Howler monkeys in the same forests select their food more deliberately, have a less diverse diet, and defecate only twice daily. As expected, they avoid plants with high alkaloid and tannin concentrations, which can vary from mildly unpalatable to highly toxic.

Strier, an anthropologist, has collected thirty foods eaten by the muriquis, including leaves, flowers, and fruits. Laboratory analysis has revealed relatively high concentrations of secondary compounds such as tannins and phenolics. When compared to the plants favored by other tropical monkeys, the muriquis consume a more chemically laden diet, but their digestion is rapid. They excrete plant toxins before they can be absorbed. Muriquis do not favor plants with lower concentrations of secondary compounds, even when they are available for selection. Clearly, they are adapted to ingest potentially toxic plants with impunity.

After reading accounts of leaf-swallowing behavior in chimpanzees and its effect on parasite levels, Strier considered the possibility that secondary compounds might also control parasites and even reproductive cycles in the muriquis. Fecal samples were examined for intestinal parasites and hormone levels, and the results suggest some remarkable interactions between the monkeys and the secondary compounds in their plant diet. Before their mating season in late October, the muriquis at Fazenda Montes Claros feed intensively on the leaves of two leguminous trees, *Apuleia leiocarpa* and *Platypodium elegans*. Apparently these plants have low levels of tannins, secondary compounds that render proteins indigestible; the leaves of these two woody legumes may serve the muriquis as a high protein food source before the exertions of their mating season. They also contain phytoestrogens, the flavonoid compounds that can increase estrogen levels and possibly control primate reproduction by decreasing fertility.

Occasionally, the muriquis extend their foraging from the central forest to the forest periphery, where they feed on the fruits of monkey ear (*Enterolobium contortisiliquum*). These leguminous trees colonize the interface between forest and pasture, and they seem to constitute only a minor food source for the muriquis. Nevertheless, the genus *Enterolobium* is well known in tropical America as a source of soap substitutes and parasite medications, the ethnobotanical uses of the steroid-containing saponins that occur in the fruit and bark. The steroids in the monkey ear fruits may serve to regulate mating and reproduction in the muriquis, possibly by promoting the synthesis of progesterone from stigmasterol, a steroid that occurs naturally in monkey ear fruits.

In addition, the muriquis at Fazenda Montes Claros revealed no parasites in their fecal samples, compared to a population at Carlos Botelho near Sao Paulo, in which almost 90 percent of the monkeys showed signs of parasite infection. An herbivorous diet rich in secondary compounds may have this incidental benefit for the muriquis; even if consumption of the medicinal plants by primates is not intentional, they very likely afford the same health benefits to muriquis and to humans.

Additional Evidence of Zoopharmacognosy

As with any new field, anecdotal observations may now begin to fit like puzzle pieces into a broader understanding of animal behavior and medicinal plants. More than twenty years ago, Holly Dublin, a scientist with the World Wildlife Fund, spent a year tracking a pregnant elephant in East Africa. She noted that the elephant's daily behavior was remarkably constant, with similar patterns of eating and walking, until the end of gestation. The elephant traveled a long distance, about twenty-eight miles, and then completely ate the leaves and woody trunk of a small tree, an African species of the borage and forget-me-not family (Boraginaceae); in four days, she bore a healthy calf. Kenyan women use a leaf tea from this tree to induce labor at the end of their pregnancies, which raises several questions. Do female elephants routinely seek this tree when birth is imminent? Did Kenyan women learn to brew their tea from observing the late gestational behavior of African elephants, or might this be just a curious coincidence? Field studies may reveal additional evidence for the use of medicinal plants by elephants and clarify the possible role of plant secondary compounds in inducing labor.

Navajo legend describes bear-root (*Ligusticum porteri*), an aromatic member of the parsley family (Umbelliferae), as a gift from North American brown bears that could be used to treat stomach aches and infection. Local lore includes descriptions of bears chewing the roots and spreading the maceration on their faces and fur, where it may protect them from external parasites and fungi. Kodiak bears in captivity exhibit the same behavior and even seem to calm themselves with the plant, suggesting that such fur-rubbing behavior is instinctive. Ethnobotanist Shawn Sigstedt has described bear-root as a fundamental medicinal plant for all Native American populations within the natural range of the plant. Bear behavior may indeed have pointed the way. Perhaps Native Americans observed bears chewing and anointing themselves with native *Ligusticum* species and thence developed their tradition for the medicinal use of bear-root. Coincidentally, a European species (*Ligusticum mutellina*) is also used for stomach complaints, while in China and Japan *L. acutilobum* is used to aid labor in childbirth.

Fur-rubbing with possible medicinal benefits also occurs in mon-

Figure 7-4. Prior to giving birth to her calf, a female African elephant was observed consuming a native tree that might have helped to induce labor.

keys. Mary Baker, an anthropologist at the University of California (Riverside), has observed white-faced capuchin monkeys in Costa Rica gathering and rubbing a variety of pungent plants into their fur; various citrus fruits (*Citrus* spp.,), a wild pepper (*Piper marginatum*), and a clematis (*Clematis dioica*) are used by capuchins engaged in this behavior. Fur-rubbing seems to increase during the warm, humid weather of the rainy season, when parasitic skin infections may be more common. All these plants have abundant secondary compounds with local folk uses for repelling insects, healing, and skin complaints, and an ointment made from the clematis is used throughout the West Indies, Central America, and South America to treat skin diseases.

Bears may also benefit from swallowing whole leaves, in a manner reminiscent of African chimpanzees that control worm infections by consuming the hairy leaves of *Aspilia*. Barrie Gilbert of Utah State University has observed Alaskan brown bears preparing for hibernation. He postulates that the occasional swallowing of whole sedge leaves (*Carex* sp.) may serve to remove tapeworms from the bears' intestines, before they settle down to a period of prolonged inactivity during which the parasites could do considerable harm to their ursine hosts. The coarse, sharp-edged leaves of sedges may serve to scrape the worms from their points of attachment in the intestines.

Disarming Toxins

Zoopharmacognosy considers the use of medicinal plants by animals, and the compounds that first evolved in plants as deterrents and toxins now may render certain plants valuable as medicines for animals and humans. As with the various insects that use botanical toxins for their defense, plants can find themselves in the unenviable position of being consumed for their particular secondary compounds.

Medicinal and defense adaptations aside, animals that can safely process and use toxic plants as foods are also at an advantage. In effect, they have an energy source that is unavailable to most others since they are able to exploit some "unusable" food resources that are toxic to their competitors, a real advantage in survival. While not zoopharmacognosy in the strict sense, the ability to disarm plant toxins still reveals biological compromise and coevolution between animal and plant species that have coexisted in the same habitats for millions of years. Possibly the secondary compounds in herbivore diets have biological functions that have not yet been detected or even imagined, or toxic plants may merely represent a food source awaiting herbivores with the necessary adaptations. Various animals have evolved strategies that allow them to deal effectively with toxins in their leafy diets.

The hoatzins of South America are chicken-sized birds that frequent floodplains, where they feed voraciously on about thirty plant species. Their diet is exclusively vegetarian and includes plants from some notoriously toxic families such as the legumes (Leguminosae), which are known for cyanogenic glycosides, and members of the cashew and mango family (Anacardiaceae), which produce urushiol, the main component of the irritant oil in poison oak and poison ivy (*Toxicodendron* spp.).

Hoatzins thrive on a leafy plant diet, digesting about 70 percent of the fiber (cellulose from plant walls) that they ingest, and they feed efficiently because there is relatively little competition for the plants that they eat. Biologically, they are the avian equivalent of cows, with a foregut that is the anatomical equivalent of a second stomach. From an ecological perspective, they fill an exclusive niche as herbivores that are able to tolerate toxic secondary compounds from plants in their diet, but the mechanism that they use to disarm the toxins is not yet known. Possibly the bacteria that normally occur in their foregut rapidly break down plant secondary compounds into innocuous molecular fragments.

In contrast to the hoatzins, birds that depend on fruits and seeds for their energy face intense competition for food resources. Unripe fruits are often astringent, bitter, or even toxic, and seeds often package toxins along with the embryo and stored food. The toxins prevent animals from eating the fruit before they are ready for dispersal and protect the seeds destined to mature into the next generation. Birds such as parrots that routinely dine on fruits and seeds face a chemical dilemma: Do they feed on unripe fruit and risk the effects of toxicity or wait until fruits ripen and contend with intense competition for the resources?

Zoologist Jared Diamond observed parrots in New Guinea engaging in geophagy, the eating of soil, and this may provide a clue how these birds detoxify fruits and seeds laden with chemicals. New Guinean parrots, hundreds of individuals belonging to five species, flocked to the site of a landslide and fed deliberately on the bare soil. The soils that they favor have high concentrations of minerals like kaolinite that bind positively charged alkaloid molecules and keep them from interfering with the parrots' physiology. A sample of New Guinea soil used by the parrots binds one-tenth of its weight with the alkaloid quinine and also can bind tannins. When parrots are fed quinine and their selected soil, the soil minerals bind to the alkaloid molecules in the birds' intestines; this decreases the alkaloid level in the parrots' blood by 60 percent, which explains why parrots can consume doses of seed toxins that would prove fatal to primates and other birds. Parrots can feast on poisonous fruits and seeds quite safely, and they have competed favorably in the evolutionary arena. They are a diverse group, with 350 species of mostly strong fliers that can travel through the forest canopy to dine exclusively on fruits and seeds, regardless of their toxic secondary compounds.

Red colobus monkeys in Tanzania exploit a similar adaptation that allows them to feast on mangoes (*Mangifera* spp.) and other foods that are high in phenols which interfere with digestion. They gather and eat charcoal from burned wood and village kilns. Phenol molecules adhere to the surface of the charcoal particles, while allowing the food proteins to be absorbed by the monkeys' intestines. Humans also use soil minerals as a defense against plant toxins in their diet, presumably a technique developed by trial and error. Sardinians traditionally used clay to prepare a nutritious bread flour from acorns with high tannin concentrations, and South American Indians eat clay along with wild potatoes (*Solanum* sp.) that are laced with toxic alkaloids, rendering the tubers safe and edible.

Domestic Strategies

Behavioral adaptations in animals include exploiting plant secondary compounds for successful nest-building and food storage. European starlings line their nests with leaves and stems of the common wild carrot (*Daucus carota*), which kills the fowl mites that try to colonize starling nests. How the starlings evolved this behavior is unknown; nest-lining and plant selection may just be a remarkable coincidence with some health benefits to the birds.

Pikas are small, mountain-dwelling mammals that store food for winter in well-constructed hay piles. They are lagomorphs, rabbit relatives, that do not hibernate but forage actively in their alpine habitats. They need a substantial food supply for the long winter and subsequent breeding season, which occurs while the alpine meadows are still snow-covered. While a graduate student at Arizona State University, Denise Dearing observed pikas in Colorado selectively haying alpine avens (*Geum* sp.), a wildflower that is a toxic food for pikas. Alpine avens, however, seems to serve another function in inhibiting bacterial breakdown in the hay piles constructed by the pikas. Pikas layer the avens plants in their hay piles instinctively, but the origin of this hay-piling behavior is also unknown. The avens can be eaten safely months later, after its secondary compounds have decomposed and its presence has helped to preserve the food stores in the hay pile through the winter months.

While not zoopharmacognosy in the strict sense, these patterns of behavior seem to decrease the likelihood of disease and enhance survival. They suggest new areas to investigate, particularly the various botanical materials used in nest building, the secondary compounds in plant tissues, and the possible role of these chemicals in the survival of animals in nature.

Reality, Interpretation, and the Methods of Science

Humans use medicinal plants; as primates we are the products of evolution, so it is not particularly surprising that animals may also benefit from the secondary compounds produced by plants. Chimpanzees are our closest extant biological relatives, and their plight is probably not very different from the situation faced by early hominids. Both were intelligent primates that relied on plants as primary food sources and lived in habitats rich with botanical diversity. Behaviors, such as leaf-swallowing and pith-eating, may have originated when tasting and experimenting with plants, resulting in a benefit of enhanced survival from disease and parasites. The use of medicinal plants may have been passed through family lines as a learned behavior or may have become encoded as instinctive behavior in chimpanzees and other species.

The new field of zoopharmacognosy is under scrutiny for its interpretation of observed animal behaviors, but critical examination is a normal part of the scientific process. Within the arena of science, peer reviewers and critics may argue against the deliberate use of medicinal plants, but the issue seems out of proportion to the obvious adaptations that have been observed in the field. Certainly no zoologist or anthropologist is proposing that primates, bears, or elephants are physicians or pharmacists. On the other hand, it does seem plausible that specific feeding behavior could be the product of natural selection. The desire to explore their botanical surroundings may have led to some medicinal coincidences for animals in their natural habitats. Chimpanzees that tended to eat certain plants might be the individuals that survived, reproduced, and passed this adaptive behavior on to their offspring, the result of medicinal properties of specific plants in their diet. If certain leaves are bad-tasting or rough-textured, it seems reasonable that they would be swallowed whole rather than chewed. This hypothesis suggests a mechanism for the origins of medicinal botany among early hominid groups, and the similarity between human and animal plant uses is particularly intriguing. The instinctive attraction to plants that have pungent or resinous qualities may be a behavioral trait that we share with primates and other animal species, which has resulted in similar botanical solutions for ailments common to animals and humans. Does this imply that the secondary compounds in animal diets are "medicines" in the strict sense, consumed intentionally to treat a particular ailment? Perhaps behavioral studies with animals in captivity will reveal more about instinctive versus learned behavior and the definition of zoopharmacognosy.

Does the premise of zoopharmacognosy violate Occam's razor, the philosophical caveat that urges scientists to be no more inventive in their explanations than their observations absolutely require? In science there is no room for fanciful theorizing that departs far from the facts at hand; the simpler of two theories is preferable, and we should try to explain new observations in terms of what is already known. Zoopharmacognosy is indeed a new explanation that ascribes essentially human behavior to animals, but the observations of animal behavior that led anthropologists and zoologists to this theory are also quite unique. Perhaps animal and human behavior will prove to be a continuum of interactions with the natural environment, including the vast botanical diversity that provides the essential backdrop for life on land.

CHAPTER 8

~

Chemical Prospecting and
New Plant Medicines

THE POTENTIAL for new medicines is a biological reality based on the huge diversity of plants available for study. Botanists estimate that there are more than 250,000 species of flowering plants, and most of this diversity still needs to be explored for its medicinal value. About 40 percent of the prescription drugs sold in the United States contain one or more components derived from plants, a proportion that will probably increase with heightened interest and research in medicinal botany. Today, however, only about forty plants are commonly used in U.S. medicine. This underuse of medicinal plants is an unfortunate symptom of "civilization," the high cost of developing new medicines and the legal questions concerning ownership of medicinal plants and the compounds that they synthesize. According to the World Health Organization, 80 percent of the global population depends primarily on traditional botanical cures, and medicine as practiced in the United States is an exception to the rule. Our limited botanical pharmacopoeia contrasts with the Asian tradition, in which folk healers use hundreds of species for specific medical problems. Even the medicine of western Europe incorporates traditional herbs into a modern context; a German physician might prescribe a synthetic antibiotic and chamomile tea to treat an ailing patient.

Nevertheless the outlook in the United States is favorable for botanical prospecting. Medicinal plants can be identified through field ethnobotany, herbarium studies, or screening of temperate and tropical plants. We may discover new medical uses for familiar plants, or we may identify new species with potential as anticancer or antiviral drugs. In the United States, government requirements for drug research and development err on the side of caution, and the resulting costs are high. Meanwhile, plants are disappearing from their natural habitats, often before they can be examined for medicinal use.

Herbal products stand in contrast to pharmaceutical drugs. Various herbal extracts, capsules, and teas have proliferated since 1994, when Congress exempted them from regulation by the Food and Drug Administration. Herbs that are marketed as nonprescription dietary supplements must be sold without claims of their medicinal effectiveness, although in the American marketplace that caveat is routinely circumvented. In Europe, perhaps the result of an ancient herbal tradition, the distinction between medicinal herbs and prescription drugs is less clear. German physicians routinely prescribe botanical cures such as valerian (*Valeriana officinalis;* Plate 28) as a sedative and feverfew (*Tanacetum parthenium*) for migraine headaches; they consider the safety and efficacy of familiar herbs to be historical and assume that any ill effects will be reported to local practitioners.

Potential hazards are introduced as the American marketplace is flooded with herbal products of undocumented origin and chemistry, some with potential toxicity and dubious claims. Poisoning with botanical compounds is a real possibility. This chapter will emphasize the future of new plant medicines in the strict sense, with attention to the secondary compounds that can be isolated from plants to treat illnesses ranging from cancer to malaria; we will consider the past, present, and future of herbalism in the final chapter.

In the United States, about one hundred drug companies are seeking new medicinal compounds from plants, but the most systematic approach to new discoveries originates with Shaman Pharmaceuticals. Backed with venture capital and committed to the development of drugs from rain forest knowledge and habitats, this company's researchers have identified more than three thousand possible new sources of drugs from nature. Teams of physicians and ethnobotanists remain on site in South America, Africa, and Southeast Asia to establish long-term relationships with healers and learn local medical tradition, and new botanical medicines that are being developed by Shaman Pharmaceuticals are in the process of clinical trials that lead to Food and Drug Administration approval. These experimental drugs include a treatment for severe diarrhea, an oral antifungal drug, and an ointment for the skin sores caused by herpes infections.

Cancer Drugs from Plants

Folk remedies for cancer have long been viewed with suspicion, in part due to the difficulty in diagnosing cases of cancer under primitive conditions. Various popular "alternative" therapies, some botanical in origin, are equally dubious; many recall the drug marketed as laetrile, an unproven cancer therapy derived from the cyanide-laden seeds of apricots (*Prunus armeniaca*). Its proponents described the compound as a "magic bullet," capable of selective destruction of cancerous cells. Unfortunately, laetrile brought false hope rather than cures, and some patients substituted laetrile for the standard treatments of surgery, chemotherapy, and radiation. Yet many plants do hold legitimate promise for cancer treatment because their second-

Figure 8-1. The seeds of apricots (*Prunus armeniaca*) produce a cyanogenic glycoside that was marketed as laetrile, an unproven cancer therapy.

ary compounds can slow or stop the growth of certain malignancies. Standard chemotherapy now includes effective botanical medicines such as vincristine, vinblastine, and paclitaxel (taxol) that have saved and prolonged the lives of cancer patients. Chemotherapy also relies on derivatives of plant secondary compounds, such as the drug etoposide that is synthesized using podophyllotoxin from the underground parts of May apple (*Podophyllum peltatum;* Plate 23).

Some phytochemicals may even have the potential to prevent cancers before they begin; an example is the compound sulforaphane, which is found in broccoli and other cultivars of *Brassica oleracea* such as kale and Brussels sprouts. Sulforaphane induces animal cells to produce the so-called phase II detoxification enzymes, proteins that remove carcinogenic compounds from a cell's interior, before cancerous growth can begin. Even low doses of sulforaphane seem to protect carcinogen-injected laboratory rats from developing cancerous tumors. Cancer protection may also be provided by resveratrol, a phytoalexin known from several food plants, including grapes (*Vitis vinifera*). Probably the first use of resveratrol originated with *kojo-kon,* an Asian folk medicine derived from the powdered roots of Japanese knotweed (*Polygonum cuspidatum*). Plants produce resveratrol in response to fungal infection or injury; its high concentration in grape skins probably protects the fruit from decomposing fungi, including the wild yeast that thrives on the outer waxy bloom of grapes. Resveratrol also seems to inhibit cancer by inducing the synthesis of enzymes that work against carcinogens in the cell. Laboratory studies show that resveratrol can stop the growth of human leukemia cells that are grown in cultures. Besides its anticancer potential, resveratrol may also be useful in controlling high levels of cholesterol and in preventing the formation of blood clots.

Genistein, a compound from soybeans (*Glycine max*), stops the progress of cancerous tumors by halting their blood supply. Tumors depend on the growth of capillaries to keep them supplied with the blood necessary for growth; genistein inhibits the growth of capillaries to small tumors, and it may have potential as a drug that could prevent the proliferation of additional tumors once a malignancy has started. Studies of local epidemiology reveal lower rates of breast and prostate cancer in populations with diets high in soybeans and soy products. Ellagic acid is yet another botanical molecule that may represent a new class of cancer-preventing drugs. It occurs in galls, nuts, and fruits and seems to counteract several malignancies, including cancers of the skin, esophagus, and liver. High concentrations of ellagic acid occur in unripe seeds and fruits, suggesting that the molecules function against fungi and pests that attack developing plant parts.

Several more phytochemicals have potential as new cancer drugs, including camptothecin from the bark of the Chinese tree of joy (*Camptotheca acuminata*), a compound first used to treat advanced cases of colorectal cancer. Marketed as Camptosar, camptothecin holds promise for several malignancies such as lung cancer and ovarian tumors. Unlike the Pacific yew, the source of paclitaxel, the trees are fast-growing, and several thousand are now in cultivation in Louisiana. Preliminary studies with *Camptotheca* seedlings suggest that environmental conditions influence the production of camptothecin; seedlings grown in the shade have higher concentrations of the medicinal alkaloid.

Trees also yield betulinic acid, another recently discovered compound that holds promise as a treatment for malignant melanoma, a common skin cancer. Betulinic acid was first isolated from the bark of an African fruit tree (*Zizyphus mauritania*), but the compound also occurs in the bark of white birch (*Betula alba*). Its specific biological function in tree bark is unknown, but it may serve as a deterrent against predators or pathogenic fungi. One favorable indication is that betulinic acid seems to be specific in its activity against the growth of melanoma cells; in contrast to camptothecin, paclitaxel, and vinblastine that are toxic to other types of cells, it does not affect the growth of nonmalignant tissue. The process of extracting betulinic acid from bark cells is relatively simple and inexpensive, unlike the complex chemical extraction of paclitaxel from yew bark, and it eventually may be incorporated into products such as sunscreens as a preventative against skin cancer.

The chemical basis of folk cures for cancer may also suggest some promising new directions for research, such as the glycosides from *Wisteria brachybotrys,* long used in Japan to treat malignancies. Even the roots of ginseng (*Panax ginseng*), among the most familiar medicinal herbs, yield a saponin-containing glycoside that acts against skin cancer induced by ultraviolet radiation. Cancer treatments from the tradition of folk medicine may lack immediate credibility because of the difficulty in diagnosing true cancers, but ethnobotanical drugs for growths and tumors may nevertheless yield some promising cancer therapies.

Plants and AIDS

Worldwide about 23 million people are infected with the human immunodeficiency virus (HIV), the pathogen that causes acquired immunodeficiency syndrome (AIDS). AIDS is a complex array of disorders resulting from the deterioration of the immune system, and infected individuals become susceptible to rare forms of cancer; common microbes become opportunistic pathogens. HIV uses cells of the immune system (macrophages and helper T cells) as sites for reproduction, and multiple copies of the viral genetic material (RNA) are made and packaged in new viral particles, ready for dispersal to new viral hosts. More cells of the immune system are killed or damaged with each round of infection, when millions of viral particles may be produced each day. Despite the production of antibodies and helper T cells that fight the disease, eventually the virus prevails, and the infections and cancers associated with AIDS begin to appear.

While no known cure or vaccine protects against HIV, drugs slow the progression of the viral infection and the onset of AIDS. New anti-HIV compounds from natural sources are reported almost daily, some essentially unproven and others with distinct promise based on *in vitro* research. Secondary compounds evolved and synthesized by plants may eventually play a significant role in combating the HIV viral infection and the AIDS infections incurred by a compromised immune system. More than thirty-six thousand extracts have been tested by the National Cancer Institute, and in laboratory studies about 10 percent of them have exhibited some anti-HIV activity.

One of the most promising anti-AIDS compounds is produced by a Malaysian tree, a member of the tropical garcinia family (Guttiferae) that is valued for its wood and resins. John Burley, a botanist at the Arnold Arboretum, first collected about two pounds of bark and branches from *Calophyllum lanigerum* growing in a swampy site in Sarawak, a Malaysian state that was once part of northern Borneo. The samples arrived at the National Cancer Institute, along with hundreds of other plant samples destined for testing. Eight compounds were isolated from the *C. lanigerum* sample, and one of them, calanolide A, showed anti-HIV activity. Chemically, calanolide A is a coumarin, and it is now being tested for toxicity in human trials; eventually it may be one of the antiviral ingredients included in AIDS "cocktails," drug mixtures that have slowed the rate of AIDS progression and extended the lives of HIV-infected patients.

When researchers at the National Cancer Institute needed more material of *Calophyllum lanigerum* for testing, a team from the University of Illinois headed by botanist Djaja Soejarta revisited the site. They found that the original tree had been cut, perhaps by a local family that used it for firewood. Extracts from similar trees nearby showed no antiviral activity, but eventually another specimen with the same chemistry was found in a botanic garden in Singapore. Soejarta continued his search for calanolide-producing trees and found that the related species *C. teysmanni* produces calanolide B, a compound that is also undergoing experimental trials as an anti-HIV drug. Rather than requiring twigs and leaves, calanolide B can be extracted from the latex that exudes from small wounds in the bark of mature trees, making it a renewable resource that can be collected by local forestry workers. If the trials progress as anticipated, the state of Sarawak will receive royalties and income as part of a joint venture leading to the successful development and marketing of the calanolide drugs. Ideally, this arrangement will encourage the local government to preserve the native forest as a long-term economic resource.

Calophyllum trees were not recognized for their antiviral activity until they were collected for laboratory screening, but bark of the rain forest tree *Homolanthus nutans* was long valued as a local remedy for hepatitis by the villagers of Falealupo in Western Samoa. Botanist Paul Allan Cox of Brigham Young University collected and sent bark specimens to the National Cancer Institute, where the antiviral compound prostratin was first isolated. Studies suggest that prostratin inhibits HIV growth and may have potential as a drug for AIDS patients. Cox negotiated an agreement with the National Cancer Institute that benefits the government of Western Samoa and the villagers of Falealupo with royalties from the marketing of prostratin, if the research yields a successful drug.

Another potential anti-HIV drug originated in Africa with a woody vine that was first collected in southwestern Cameroon in 1987. Working for the Missouri Botanical Garden and the National Cancer Institute, botanist Duncan Thomas found an *Ancistrocladus* species twining up a tree in the Korup National Park near the capital city of Yaounde; he noted its distinct leaves and collected several kilograms of leaves and stems for National Cancer Institute researchers. A crude extract of the *Ancistrocladus* vine yielded michellamine B, a new alkaloid that in initial trials seemed to work against the HIV virus, including strains that have developed immunity to other drugs. A few years later, botanists from the Missouri Botanical Garden could not locate the original vine, but Thomas returned to Cameroon, found more specimens of the original plant, and collected additional leaves and bark for the National Cancer Institute. The vine has since been named *Ancistrocladus korupensis,* a new African species found only near the Korup National Park in Cameroon.

Michellamine B is a chemically stable molecule present in the leaves even after they have fallen from the vines. Sufficient michellamine B for testing is contained in *Ancistrocladus* leaves that litter the forest floor, which may protect the limited number of wild vines from destruction by harvesting. The vines vary in their concentrations of michellamine B, and the high-yielding varieties are being propagated, ready for large-scale cultivation if the initial trials are successful. Experimental field plots with several thousand propagated plants will reveal whether *Ancistrocladus* vines are best grown in sun, shade, or forest habitats, in fertile or depleted soil.

Several other botanical drugs may be useful in treating AIDS-related infections and cancers. The alkaloid berberine is found in several plants, including members of the poppy family (Papaveraceae), and has been used to treat infections caused by bacteria, fungi, and protozoans. As a broad-spectrum antibiotic with few side effects, berberine has potential for treating the various forms of severe diarrhea associated with AIDS. Protozoans in particular cause gastrointestinal infections in people with damaged immune systems, and perhaps a maintenance dose of berberine would help to control such opportunistic pathogens.

AIDS patients also find themselves at risk for cancers that are usually controlled by a normal immune system. Vinorelbine, a semisynthetic version of one anticancer alkaloid from *Catharanthus roseus,* disrupts the spindle fibers that are responsible for separating chromosomes during cell division. It works at lower concentrations and with fewer side effects than the alkaloids derived directly from the plants, and it could be useful in combating Kaposi's sarcoma, a rare skin cancer associated with AIDS.

Botanical Antibiotics

Egyptian healers knew that a blue-green mold placed on a wound could prevent infection; they had discovered the antibiotic properties and practical medicinal uses of the *Penicillium* fungus long before Western knowledge of penicillin for treating bacterial diseases. In nature, *Penicillium* antibiotics destroy the other microorganisms that compete with the fungus for the same food sources, and they represent a survival strategy that evolved to eliminate their competitors. For years we have relied on antibiotics, but the need for new antibiotic compounds to treat human disease is acute, as more pathogenic bacteria develop immunity to existing drugs such as penicillin. Antibiotics do not have to originate with fungi; some green plants also produce antibiotic secondary compounds that may have evolved to control the microorganisms that cause plant diseases.

Botanical antibiotics are abundant in the natural world, and some are now used to a limited extent. Eventually these may provide alternatives for some fungal and synthetic antibiotics. Examples abound: Chaulmoogra oil from trees in the genera *Hydnocarpus* and *Tarakto-genos* contains hydnocarpic and chaulmoogric acids, antibiotics that work against the bacterium that causes leprosy. Various members of the mustard family (Cruciferae) produce compounds that are antibiotic to both major groups of bacteria, Gram-positive cells and Gram-negative cells alike. Juglone from black walnut (*Juglans nigra*) has been used to treat fungal infections of the skin, and creosote bush (*Larrea divaricata*) has been used to treat skin infections and venereal disease.

Louis Pasteur described the antibacterial properties of garlic in 1858, and historically garlic has been used to treat infections such as colds and tuberculosis. The antibiotic compounds produced by garlic may offer another option for treating current antibiotic-resistant cases of tuberculosis. Garlic (*Allium sativum*) yields alliin and allicin,

Figure 8-2. Garlic (*Allium sativum*) is a source of pungent antibiotic compounds that are effective against bacteria and fungi.

sulfur-containing compounds that act against a range of bacteria and fungi. The role of the volatile garlic chemicals in nature is to deter insects and other predators; tissue damage sets off a series of chemical reactions in garlic cells in which an enzyme converts alliin to allicin, releasing its characteristic sharp odor and strong taste. Allicin is antibiotic against bacteria such as *Staphylococcus* and *Salmonella,* and tons of garlic were used in field dressings to prevent sepsis during both world wars. Garlic-derived compounds are now used as antibiotics for chickens and cattle and as pesticides that eliminate mosquito larvae, nematode worms, and parasites such as lice and intestinal worms.

Sanguinarine, an alkaloid from bloodroot (*Sanguinaria canadensis;* Plate 24), inhibits the growth of oral bacteria and is used in toothpaste and mouthwash to prevent bacterial plaque formation on teeth. It is related to berberine, an alkaloid known from goldenseal (*Hydrastis canadensis;* Plate 19) and several other species. Berberine acts against bacteria and protozoans, such as those that cause malaria and the intestinal infections associated with AIDS. New antimalarial antibiotics are important as *Plasmodium* strains become increasingly immune to quinine and similar compounds such as chloroquinine that originated with *Cinchona* trees. New medicines are needed to treat malaria worldwide, and there are several botanical possibilities. Betulinic acid, the bark compound that can be used to treat melanomas, also inhibits *Plasmodium* reproduction.

Chinese researchers have investigated artemisinin, a terpene isolated from the leaves of wormwood (*Artemisia annua*), as another new antimalarial medicine. The suggestion to investigate wormwood for antimalarial activity came from Chinese herbal medicine; wormwood is the *qing hao* that was prescribed for fevers by the Chinese physician Li Shi-zen in 1527. First isolated in 1972, the compound artemisinin has been the basis for several semi-synthetic drugs that have greater solubility in vaccines and greater antimalarial activity. Artemisinin is now used as an alternative to chloroquinine in areas of China with resistant strains of *Plasmodium,* and it is also being investigated in the United States as a drug of particular interest to the military, since malaria can quickly debilitate troops. Questions remain about how quickly malaria will evolve immunity to artemisinin; in fact, the best defense against malaria would be an effective vaccine, which eventually may also have a botanical component. Stimulon, derived from the bark of the South American tree *Quillaja saponaria,* is an ingredient in an experimental malaria vaccine. Stimulon seems to work as an adjuvant, a pharmacological additive that improves the effectiveness of a vaccine in promoting the formation of antibodies.

Early antibiotic claims also surrounded the essential oil derived from Australian tea trees (*Melaleuca alternifolia*). During the nineteenth century, the Ti Ta Volatile Oil Company of Brisbane advertised that their product Ti Ta "cures all disease." That was an unlikely claim, but for many years tea tree oil has been used topically to treat carbuncles and other skin infections, and its long use in patent medicines and skin treatments suggests that it may be effective. During the first half of the twentieth century, it seemed to be a good alternative to carbolic acid, a popular germicide that could damage tissues, but with the development of antibiotics during World War II, the use of tea tree oil to treat bacterial infections virtually ceased. Until the 1930s, it was standard issue in all first-aid kits used by the Australian military.

There has been recent interest in using tea tree oil to treat conditions ranging from acne, herpes, and cystitis to arthritis and muscle pain. Tons of the oil are produced annually for export, but its precise efficacy and toxicity remain unknown. The Food and Drug Administration allows the addition of tea tree oil to topical preparations for fragrance, but no therapeutic claims for the oil have been approved. Nevertheless, tea tree oil may deserve clinical investigation for potential use as a mild topical antiseptic. It is effective in killing the antibiotic-resistant strains of bacteria such as *Staphylococcus aureus* that lurk in hospitals; researchers at the University of East London are continuing their study of the use of tea tree oil against hospital-dwelling bacterial strains. Clean hands are important in preventing the spread of bacterial disease, and tea tree oil may prove useful as a safe, effective hand disinfectant for medical practitioners.

Plants and the Mind

Botanical medicines treat physical ailments, from cancer to chronic pain, and offer hope for afflictions of the brain. Traditional Chinese herbal medicine recommends leaf preparations of *Ginkgo biloba* as beneficial to brain function, and this tradition has integrated into modern European medicine. In Europe, an elderly person might find a local physician recommending ginkgo leaf extracts to control symptoms of aging such as forgetfulness and poor circulation or even the more serious symptoms of Alzheimer's disease. The trees have a complex chemistry; besides various flavones and glycosides, ginkgo trees produce unique secondary compounds known as ginkgolides. These twenty-carbon compounds form a molecular "cage" capable of binding ions or molecules with positive surface charges. Ginkgolide compounds increase the capillary blood flow in patients suffering from circulatory problems, and in one study, ginkgo extracts improved mental function in young subjects and elderly patients suffering from circulatory diseases. Recent studies suggest that ginkgo can help some patients with Alzheimer's disease to regain several months of lost cognitive ability, but unlike other drugs available to treat Alzheimer's disease, ginkgo extracts are not effective in all cases.

Young and old alike may be affected by melancholia, from mild seasonal afflictions to deep depression. Depression is certainly not a modern condition, nor is the search for medicines that can improve mental well-being a recent pursuit. The herbalist John Gerard recommended borage (*Borago officinalis*) "for the comfort of the hart, for the driving away of sorrowe, and increasing the joie of the minde" and creeping buttercup (*Ranunculus repens*) for a person who is "lunatike in the waine of the moon." Various lady's slipper orchids (*Cypri-*

pedium spp.) were used for sedation and despondency, first by Native Americans as a root decoction for mental afflictions and hysteria and later as a common nineteenth-century treatment for "nerves."

Lady's slipper orchids were also known as American valerian, a reference to *Valeriana officinalis* (Plate 28), a European herb that is now a common ingredient in nonprescription tranquilizers. The active ingredients of valerian are the valepotriates, terpenes that affect the central nervous system by controlling agitation and by serving as a stimulant for fatigue. Valerian has been used to treat depression, insomnia, and hypochondria, and it is now an active ingredient in dozens of nonprescription sedatives that are marketed in Europe. The nineteenth-century Shakers in Enfield, New Hampshire, prepared and sold Brown's Extract of English Valerian, for "Nervousness, Lowness of Spirits, Debility . . . Hysteria, Restlessness . . . and every other disease arising from mental affection and nervous exhaustion." Forgotten in the United States for many years, valerian will likely again become a popular over-the-counter remedy for cases of mild or moderate depression.

St. John's wort (*Hypericum perforatum*) is another European herb with an ancient past and future prospects. European herbalists recommended it for healing wounds and as a mild sedative. Across the Atlantic, Native Americans used North American species of *Hypericum* for wounds and severe pain. Long associated with Balder, the Norse god of light, St. John's wort

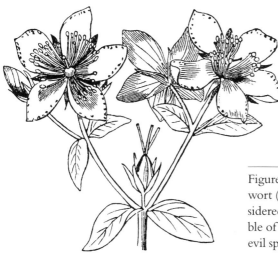

Figure 8-3. Since ancient times, St. John's wort (*Hypericum perforatum*) has been considered a plant with special properties, capable of curing melancholia and warding off evil spirits.

acquired its name during the advent of Christianity when Balder's Day became St. John's Day; the plant was believed to ward off evil spirits and have special curative properties. The species synthesizes several secondary compounds, including flavonoids, tannins, and essential oils, but the complex molecule hypericin seems to be responsible, at least in part, for its properties as an antidepressant. Extracts prepared from the flowers and leaves of St. John's wort have been widely used in Europe to treat mild to moderate cases of depression and insomnia, and clinical trials seem to support its efficacy with few side effects.

In the United States, St. John's wort is not yet a standard medical treatment, but extracts are available, and the plant appears in tea mixtures that imply an improved mental state in their advertising. Antiviral activity in St. John's wort is also a possibility, based on studies in the United States and Israel. Hypericin and the related compound pseudohypericin act against retroviruses such as HIV and may be useful in controlling AIDS. In either case, standardized doses of hypericin would seem a wise option, but herbal teas and extracts marketed as food supplements can vary widely in their chemistry. Another caveat arises from the observation that the secondary compounds of St. John's wort cause photosensitivity in cattle; there may be a similar effect in humans, suggesting that caution is in order to avoid high doses when using these products.

Kava is a narcotic beverage prepared from the dried roots and underground stems of the tropical vine *Piper methysticum,* a close relative of black pepper (*P. nigrum*). It has properties that have been known for thousands of years, and like taro (*Colocasia antiquorum*), kava was carried by canoe throughout the South Pacific by islanders who valued it for their communal rituals. It has since received attention as a potential antianxiety medication, and ethnobotanical observations suggest that small doses result in feelings of euphoria and friendliness. The active ingredients methysticin and kawain constitute 3 to 4 percent of the kava roots and underground stems. Commission E, the German government panel that reviews herbal remedies, has approved kava as effective for treating stress and anxiety; in Germany, kava is used as an herbal extract that can substitute for the synthetic drugs that are used to curb anxiety. Capsules advertised as containing standardized doses of the secondary compounds are now marketed in the United States as food supplements. These extracts also serve as muscle relaxants and seem to work in the same region of the brain to control anxiety as prescription drugs, but clinical trials are needed to assess the effects completely. On the side of caution, it should be noted that large doses of kava can be intoxicating, and side effects include allergic reactions and skin damage or yellowing.

If kava eventually becomes a pharmaceutical drug, it will be a treatment that had an early origin in the island cultures of the South Pacific. It was carried as far north as the Hawaiian Islands, where local people used it for debility and sleeplessness. The preparation ritual involved chewing or pounding the roots and underground stems, mixing in water, straining, and heating the resulting decoction. Hawaiian islanders called it *awa* and used the plant to treat sore muscles and severe headaches; even idyllic island life might include an element of stress, and the Polynesians' legacy to us might be a botanical cure for a human condition that we hold in common.

Future Prospects

The patterns of medicinal botany are clear: Discoveries are frequent, but the laboratory testing and clinical trials constitute a daunting course that private drug companies are sometimes reluctant to assume. Thousands of extracts are tested to find one new botanical medicine that is effective and sufficiently nontoxic to allow its use as a therapy. The options for research are many, and "old" plants such as St. John's wort now demand as much attention as plants new to medical science. Another such example are the cannabinoid molecules of marijuana (*Cannabis sativa;* Plate 11) that present a range of medicinal possibilities, including relief of high internal eye pressure caused by glaucoma. At low doses, cannabinoids may enhance function of the immune system, and at higher doses they may suppress it. Another secondary compound of *Cannabis,* cannabidiol, may be useful in treating the damage caused to brain tissue by strokes. As an antioxidant that neutralizes free radicals (reactive molecules of oxygen), cannabidiol may be able to stop the stroke-related damage such as paralysis and loss of speech that may be caused by free radicals released during strokes. Free radicals may also have a link to degenerative conditions such as Alzheimer's disease and Parkinson's disease, and cannabidiol may have a role in treating these conditions. Based on its recreational use, little is known of the specific marijuana secondary compounds; that knowledge will only come from clinical trials of individual *Cannabis* chemicals.

Besides research on the antimalarial properties of the genus *Artemisia,* Chinese herbal medicine offers many more areas for investigation that extend beyond the paradigms of Western medicine. Traditional healing as practiced in China incorporates millennia of experience with human ills and hundreds of medicinal plants into a body of knowledge that has been largely ignored outside Asia. Chinese physicians frequently use complex plant mixtures; sorting out the secondary compounds and their complex interactions will be a challenge, but the results will probably lead to some useful new therapies. Research in Japan suggests that one such herbal formula known as *sho-saiko-to* helps to prevent liver cancers in patients with cirrhosis. Traditional methods that rely on individual species also suggest possible methods of research: Chinese physicians use club mosses such as *Huperzia serrata* to brew teas that contain the alkaloid huperzine A; these teas have long been used to treat memory loss, and they may prove useful in treating Alzheimer's disease. Kudzu (*Pueraria thunbergiana*) is used in China to treat alcoholism, and in laboratory trials the compound daidzen isolated from kudzu does suppress alcohol consumption. The Chinese cucumber plant (*Trichosanthes kirilowii*) is the source of trichosanthin, now used as an alternative AIDS therapy and traditionally used in China to treat tumors and immune disorders. The protein MAP 30 isolated from bitter melon

(*Momordica charantia*), another member of the Cucurbitaceae, may act against HIV by inhibiting activity of the enzyme that inserts viral DNA into the host cell.

New botanical medicines may begin as "herbal remedies," taken traditionally as teas and extracts and later better understood for their chemistry and range of medicinal uses. The early use of opium and Madagascar periwinkle illustrate this sort of pattern; both were first marketed as popular patent medicines, and only later did their complex chemistry and full medicinal potential become known. Opium was first used as a crude extract in tonics and elixirs, but now it is a controlled prescription drug with dosages and effects as an analgesic that are well understood. The Madagascar periwinkle was first marketed as a patent medicine for diabetes, and only later did its alkaloids become important in cancer chemotherapy. Global exchange of information and new respect for ethnobotanical knowledge will move the work of medicinal botany forward, and over time many more poorly known secondary compounds will become valued pharmaceutical medicines.

CHAPTER 9

~

Protecting Medicinal Biodiversity and Knowledge

HOW MANY medicinal plants do we know and use? Botanists and plant chemists agree that many more medicinal compounds await discovery in forests, prairies, and hedgerows worldwide. Until then, many secondary compounds will continue to exist in nature as potential medicines awaiting discovery, but how many will be found before the plants that produce them disappear from the landscape? As habitats are changed by human activity, more species will become rare and endangered, taking with them the genes that specify their unique chemistry. Preserving a few individuals of each species is not always the answer because all plants in a species are not necessarily identical in their chemistry. Plant populations can be genetically diverse, and even within a single species there can be dramatic variations in the production of secondary compounds. The loss of genetic diversity can translate into the loss of new medicines because the plant populations that are lost may coincidentally be those that produce high concentrations of a medicinal molecule.

Extinction is a global problem, and tropical and temperate habitats alike are suffering losses of botanical diversity. Peter Raven, director of the Missouri Botanical Garden, estimates that possibly sixty thousand plant species will disappear by the middle of the twenty-first century, and tropical plants are particularly vulnerable. Tropical forests support more species than their temperate equivalents, and one species may be represented by just a few individuals within a plot of several acres. Despite their lush growth and immense stature, rain forests do not easily regenerate once they have been cut and cleared for fuel, wood products, or agricultural land. The shallow soil is often nutrient poor and does not provide a bank of viable seeds that will sprout into new saplings. Tropical forest plants have not evolved seed dormancy, and when a forest is removed, the landscape is drastically changed. Animals, including pollinators, disappear as their habitats are irreversibly changed. The plants that remain may be left without reliable pollinators and the ability to set seed for the next generation of forest plants.

Worldwide efforts to preserve biodiversity come together at meetings such as the International Consultation on the Conservation of Medicinal Plants held in Chiang Mai, Thailand, in 1988. Sponsored by the World Health Organization (WHO), International Union for the Conservation of Nature (IUCN), and the World Wide Fund for Nature (WWF), this conference focused on the loss of medicinal plant diversity as it affects traditional and modern medicine. The Chiang Mai Declaration called on people worldwide to "save the plants that save lives," with particular concern for the medicinal plants needed for primary health care in developing countries. Most of the world's population relies on native medicinal plants for healing, and local healers cannot ply their craft when native plants vanish. Moreover, if we are to share medicinal biodiversity with future generations, we need to protect not only plant species but also their habitats and pollinators.

Tropical Conservation

Botanist and explorer Alexander von Humboldt (1769–1859) referred to rain forests as the great "Hylaea," tremendous evergreen forests with a minimum rain fall of approximately eighty inches per year and a warm mean temperature of 75°F or higher. Various types of tropical forests cover about 7.75 billion acres of the earth's surface, and they provide habitats for about 125,000 species of seed plants. Deforestation around the equator has continued apace over the past several decades, as trees are felled for their wood and lands are cleared for agriculture. Asian timber companies in particular have sought forest resources from Central America, the Congo Basin, and the South Pacific; national governments willingly enter into logging contracts, and then the heavy equipment trundles into local forests to begin clearing trees. Management techniques such as selective cutting of trees and road construction with minimum forest destruction are rarely practiced. Asian logging firms now control more than half of the 21.5 million acres of government forests in Papua New Guinea and 30 million acres in the Amazon Basin.

"Slash and burn" clearing has been practiced by large logging and farming operations and by cattle ranches that use thousands of acres as agriculture fields and grazing land. Even small-scale farming results in considerable habitat loss, as a growing number of families clear agricultural plots and scavenge for fuel. Well over half of all tropical forests have now been destroyed, and as human populations continue to increase in many tropical countries, the pressure for forest resources continues to intensify. After the shallow soils are depleted, cleared lands are soon abandoned and left fallow. Tropical plants and animals do not recolonize to form new forest ecosystems on these deforested sites; instead, the bare soil is left to harden in the sun and erode in the rain.

Renewed interest in traditional agricultural practices may help to save some remaining tropical forests because farming can be done in an intact forest setting. Without removing the standing tree canopy, plants can be cultivated as shrub and herbaceous layers in the shade of the large trees, which avoids clear-cutting and soil erosion. Valuable cash crops such as shade-grown coffee can be grown in forest plantations that allow native plants, insects, birds, and other animals to live in a relatively undisturbed habitat. Such sustainable systems of agriculture incorporate a mixed community of many plant species, rather than the monoculture of modern agricultural fields of corn and wheat. Diverse habitats provide fewer opportunities for the pests and diseases that thrive in agricultural fields lacking natural diversity. Medicinal plants used in traditional healing can be encouraged to grow in these sustainable agricultural habitats, so that local forests become semi-cultivated sites that include many useful and economically important plants. Protecting the remaining tropical forests from clear-cutting will also allow the survival of plants with unknown medicinal or ethnobotanical uses.

The need to protect unknown medicinal plants has been a frequent argument for rain forest conservation. Certainly examples such as the Malaysian *Calophyllum* tree support the contention that many medicinal plants remain undiscovered in tropical forests. The calanolide compounds from *Calophyllum* slow the progress of HIV infections, but the trees had no known ethnobotanical uses and were only discovered during the screening of Malaysian plants at the National Cancer Institute. Examples like this lead to the obvious question: How many more plant medicines remain to be discovered in tropical forests?

Michael Balick, a botanist, and Robert Mendelsohn, an economist, have offered a projection based on several variables. Estimating the number of tropical plant species at 125,000, they considered how many plant parts and how many possible chemical extractions could be done for each species. They estimated three plant parts (such as roots, stems, and leaves) and two extractions for each plant part, resulting in a total of 750,000 potential chemical extracts from plants that grow in tropical forests. They multiplied the number of extracts by the number of screenings for effectiveness against various diseases and conditions that could be conducted if the extracts were shared by laboratories. Balick and Mendelsohn estimated the number of screenings at 500, suggesting that as time allows 375 million drug tests could be performed using rain forest plants. Perhaps one in a million drug tests leads to the discovery and marketing of a new plant-based medicine, so they concluded that there are potentially 375 drugs from tropical forests. Tropical forests already yield about 50 known plant medicines, leaving well over 300 that await discovery for the investment of time and money. The remaining forests will provide the plants for medicinal screening, but that assumes that forest plants survive long enough for collection and testing. The stewardship of tropical forests most often lies with the national and local governments of developing countries that daily face the constraints of poverty and overpopulation. Too often the immediate financial rewards of deforestation outweigh the long-term wisdom of forest conservation.

The key to halting tropical deforestation and the loss of medicinal plants is certainly based on economic need. Clear-cutting of forests has immediate financial rewards, so only immediate financial compensation can persuade equatorial countries to stop clear-cutting, promote sustainable agriculture, and preserve their remaining forests as valuable nonrenewable resources. Pharmaceutical companies need to pay local governments for the right to collect plants for screening, and the profits from exploration and drug development must be shared fairly with local people in the lands in which medicinal plants originate. How this will be accomplished merits consideration: Will compensation be made to national governments, townships, or local villagers? Will payments take the form of cash, medical assistance, or economic incentives? How can promises of compensation best be used to promote conservation?

The investment in time and money to develop a new drug is high, usually one or two decades of research and more than two million dollars from the initial stages of research to manufacture and marketing. The financial rewards are also high; each year we spend billions of dollars worldwide on pharmaceutical medicines, mostly on drugs that are marketed and used in Western countries. If we expect rain forests to survive and pharmaceutical exploration to continue, we must be willing to share fairly when using the natural resources of tropical countries. Only then will the surviving pharmacopoeia of medicinal plants be available for us and future generations.

Temperate Conservation

We think of temperate forests as a vast, renewable resource that can survive cycles of clearing, farming, and regeneration. Occasionally, attention is directed to the loss of a temperate species, such as the demise of American chestnut trees from an introduced parasitic fungus, but most temperate forest trees are taken for granted. Not too many years ago, Pacific yews were burned as trash trees during the logging of old-growth areas in the Pacific Northwest; with the discovery of paclitaxel (taxol) through laboratory screening, the trees evolved rapidly from forest refuse into a valuable source of a new anticancer drug.

Removing bark for paclitaxel extraction results in tree death. Pacific yew trees were clearly at risk when paclitaxel was first licensed to Bristol-Myers Squibb as part of a joint research project with the National Cancer Institute and knowledge of its efficacy spread. Paclitaxel is not a cure, but it slows the progressive growth of many malignant tumors that do not respond to other treatments, and cancer patients were eager for the product. There was immediate concern for the protection of the remaining Pacific yews and research to identify alternative sources of paclitaxel. Paclitaxel was needed for clinical trials and experimentation, and in 1991 Bristol-Myers Squibb estimated that it would need the bark from thirty-eight thousand trees for paclitaxel research. Six mature trees were needed to provide paclitaxel sufficient to treat one patient, but the existing old-growth trees needed preservation as a natural resource that would provide seeds for future generations.

This predicament bred conflict among conservationists, cancer patients, physicians, and proponents of biomedical research, those who considered the old-growth forests untouchable and patients and their advocates who needed a natural product with the potential for saving human lives. The early debate was complicated by the presence of the endangered spotted owl in the same habitats. Both the owl and the yew were protected by the Endangered Species Act, but many cancer patients viewed this as a legal complication that placed human lives at risk. Conservationists urged the long view; Wendell Wood of the Oregon Natural Resources Council told the *New York Times* in April 1991, "Our concern is that we not kill the goose that laid the golden egg. Ancient forests that gave us the yew may give us answers to medical problems we haven't thought to ask."

Attention has now turned away from using Pacific yews as the primary source of paclitaxel, at least for the present. French scientists have developed an alternative method of producing paclitaxel starting with a related compound found in the needles European yews (*Taxus baccata*), an easily renewable resource. Using the compound DAB III as a starting point, paclitaxel and the related anticancer compound docetaxel (Taxotere) can be made efficiently in the laboratory using a semisynthetic process. Several other research groups are working on various aspects of paclitaxel synthesis; a research group at the University of Leicester in England has been using hedge clippings from the large yew maze at Longleat House in Wiltshire for additional experiments in synthesizing paclitaxel from taxicin, a related compound. Pacific yews have been preserved by two serendipitous developments: the similar chemistry of related yews and the successful laboratory research that has lead to paclitaxel production from related compounds. Eventually European yews and Pacific yews may be planted as cash

Figure 9-1. The European yew (*Taxus baccata*) has potential as a renewable resource for paclitaxel which can be synthesized from the related compounds produced by this species.

crops to supply a growing demand for paclitaxel or its chemical precursors, and other yew species may also become commercial sources of the drug.

The stories of most other North American medicinal plants began less dramatically with their early medicinal uses by Native Americans. Many plants used by Native Americans became known to early European settlers, and some of these are now herbs that are mass-marketed as extracts, capsules, and teas. The loss of native medicinal plants from North American habitats now looms as a significant problem, aggravated by the renewed interest in medicinal herbs and the demand for "wildcrafted" rather than cultivated herbal products. Several species are now endangered because of their popularity in America and Europe as herbal remedies. Native North American wildflowers such as coneflower (*Echinacea* spp.) and goldenseal (*Hydrastis canadensis*) are at high risk for poaching, which may result in the disappearance of entire populations.

Long recognized as medicinal herbs, *Echinacea* species were used by the Plains Indians for various ailments including colds, burns, snakebites, and cancers. Early European settlers learned about its medicinal properties, and now *Echinacea* is a popular herbal remedy in western Europe and the United States. Of the nine species in the genus, the usual medicinal species are *E. purpurea* (Plate 16), *E. angustifolia,* and *E. pallida,* but herb collectors may also gather and combine related coneflower species from wild populations. When coneflower is sold as a dried herb, the product frequently contains a mixture of *Echinacea* species, probably with varying medicinal properties and potency. Entire populations of *Echinacea* species have been harvested from public and private lands, amounting to theft of thousands of plants and environmental vandalism. Coneflowers are easily cultivated in fields, but unscrupulous herb collectors still seek wild plants. The popularity of coneflowers as medicinal herbs has endangered the Tennessee purple coneflower (*E. tennesseensis*), a rare plant that is known from just a few populations and is federally listed as an endangered species.

Since the late nineteenth century, populations of goldenseal (*Hydrastis canadensis;* Plate 19) have gradually disappeared from forests in the eastern United States. The Cherokee and Iroquois used goldenseal for ailments ranging from dyspepsia to cancer, and a tea has been recommended variously as an herbal cure for eye infections, jaundice, inflammation of mucous membranes, and bronchitis. Medicinally, goldenseal functions as a sedative and to lower blood pressure, and it contains the antibiotic berberine and other related alkaloids. In *Medicinal Plants* (1892), Charles Millspaugh noted that goldenseal was "now becoming quite rare in this State (N.Y.)," presumably from overcollection of the underground stems and roots. Wild populations suffer when collectors overharvest the underground parts and no buds remain to grow into the mature plants that will maintain the population.

Native Americans had an extensive pharmacopoeia of North American medicinal plants that they gathered from wild populations. They needed only sufficient plant material to prepare medicines for their use, and their pharmacopoeia persisted as wild plant populations in nature that were available for use when they were needed. The commercial herb market in North America has drastically increased the pressures on wild plant populations, especially the wildflowers that are now marketed as herbal cures. The demand for wild-dug plants remains high, and temperate populations and species continue to disappear as a result of overcollection and habitat loss.

Efforts such as Save the Goldenseal launched by Frontier Cooperative Herbs in Iowa may help to protect wild plants and the cultivation of medicinal herbs. These modern herbalists have tried to correct the notion that goldenseal will mask the appearance of illicit drugs in urine samples, a damaging fallacy that has driven the wholesale price of goldenseal to more than one hundred dollars per pound. The Save the Goldenseal project also encourages propagation to replenish wild goldenseal populations and cultivation to supply medicinal demands.

Even species that are no longer in medical demand still suffer the effects of their earlier popularity. During the nineteenth century, native orchids such as the yellow lady's slipper (*Cypripedium calceolus* var. *pubescens;* Plate 15) were known as nerveroots and valued by Native Americans and European settlers to treat depression and despondency. They became part of the herbal tradition of the Shakers, who gathered the roots of yellow lady's slipper orchids from New England meadows and woods to use as a cure for nervous headaches. The plants were even marketed on the American western frontier; George Halleck Center, a nineteenth-century herbalist and medicine showman, combined yellow lady's slipper as one ingredient in his Center's Nerve Capsules. Orchid populations disappeared from overharvesting during the nineteenth century, and today the plants remain rare in their original habitats. The reproductive biology of native orchids is poorly understood; their minute seeds are dustlike, and the plants depend on symbiotic soil fungi and undisturbed habitats for their survival. In a hundred years, yellow lady's slippers have not recovered from their popularity in the American medical marketplace.

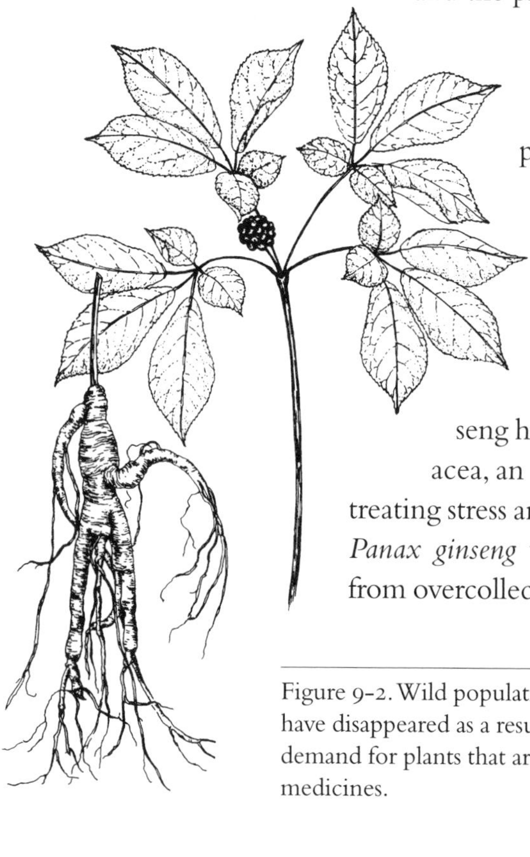

The Asian demand for ginseng foreshadowed the current interest in temperate medicinal herbs. In Asia, ginseng has long been regarded as a panacea, an adaptogenic herb essential for treating stress and many physical ailments, and *Panax ginseng* virtually disappeared in Asia from overcollection. To supply the Asian mar-

Figure 9-2. Wild populations of ginseng (*Panax quinquefolius*) have disappeared as a result of overcollection to supply the demand for plants that are common ingredients in Chinese medicines.

ket, collection of the closely related *P. quinquefolius* (Plate 22) from American forests began before 1720 and resulted in the loss of most wild ginseng populations in the United States. Colonists supplemented their incomes by collecting and drying ginseng roots. Our native ginseng is now one of six North American medicinal plants listed by the 1975 Convention on International Trade in Endangered Species in Wild Fauna and Flora (CITES), an international treaty that regulates trade for plants and animals threatened by commercial demand. Most American ginseng is shipped to Hong Kong, where it is used in various traditional Chinese medicines. As a result of market demand, the collection of wild ginseng continues as a lucrative activity, despite the availability of cultivated ginseng from farms in Wisconsin and other states. Unfortunately, a pound of wild-grown American ginseng can be sold to Asian buyers for five hundred dollars, frequently three times the price of cultivated ginseng. Along with the U.S. Fish and Wildlife Service and the U.S. Department of Agriculture, states monitor their wild ginseng populations, but there are frequent violations by herb collectors in the areas where a few wild plants remain.

Preserving Knowledge

The practical use of medicinal plants is as old as the human species; ancient texts describe the plants that were used for specific ailments and the methods for their preparation and use. Similarly, the conservation of medicinal plants is not a new problem; evidence suggests that ancient Greeks and Romans may have used the juice of silphium (*Ferula* sp.) as a contraceptive, but this valued Mediterranean species was collected into extinction. When plants are in high demand as sources of medicines, they are often at risk of disappearing from their natural habitats. Furthermore, we do not know how many other medicinal plants may have disappeared during prehistory with knowledge of their use. Plant survival and medicinal knowledge are closely linked, a huge resource of information about afflictions and cures; when plants disappear, their uses are quickly forgotten. Thousands of years of traditional medicine can disappear quickly through lack of awareness of its value, which provides the immediate motivation of ethnobotanists: To record the botanical knowledge of indigenous peoples before their information vanishes as a result of cultural change. Traditional practices may be abandoned when Western ways are introduced; in cultures where no written accounts exist, the remaining medicinal knowledge may be held by only a few older men or women who may not be able to train a successor.

Traditionally, oral accounts of valued medicinal plants have been passed through generations, and this information is often the most important to preserve. Shamans practice medicine in regions with the highest botanical biodiversity, habitats that are now often disrupted by deforestation and loss of species; the high diversity and genetic variation translate into chemical diversity and variations in individual chemistry. The tropics house a tremendous resource of potential medicines as secondary compounds, and local healers have tinkered with this diversity for millennia and refined their knowledge. As we have mentioned before, if a healer dies before training a successor to share his or her expertise, these volumes of information and experience are lost. Also, when healing tradition becomes disvalued or cast aside, the encyclopedic practical information of a single shaman can disappear with lack of interest in its continuity.

We should never discount the knowledge of "primitive" indigenous peoples. Richard Evans Schultes has documented the vast botanical information held by the local tribes that he knew during nearly five decades in South America. The Kofán and Witoto Indians of the Amazon Basin possess acute botanical skills and are able to recognize plant varieties that are indistinguishable even to observant taxonomic botanists with graduate training. The Indians are able to distinguish plant varieties with distinct chemical properties; Schultes's field notes document more than fifteen hundred plant species that are used by Amazonian tribes as medicines, narcotics, or poisons, mostly chemically unknown. These plants are still used by the Kofán and Witoto Indians, who have survived waves of "civilization" and exploitation, including generations of missionaries, Spanish colonists, rubber workers, loggers, and petroleum bosses. Their original populations have been vastly depleted as a result of harsh treatment and disease carried in by outsiders.

Although they are not chemists, Amazonian Indians know the practical synergistic effects of various plant chemicals when they are consumed together, for instance, the plants that are combined with *Banisteriopsis caapi* to make the hallucinogenic drink *ayahuasca*. Its psychoactive properties result from beta-carboline alkaloids whose properties can be enhanced by plants that produce tryptamines, a class of hallucinogenic alkaloids. The Indians have discovered two rain forest plants that work synergistically with *Banisteriopsis,* and they use leaves from *Diplopterys cabrerana* and *Psychotria viridis* to enhance the hallucinogenic properties of *ayahuasca.* Whether this has medical significance is unknown, but it reveals the depth of practical local knowledge of plant chemistry. The Kofán in particular have tremendous practical knowledge of plant toxins, and they prepare complex arrow poison mixtures that are unknown to other tribes and which may have medical significance. Yet the loss of indigenous knowledge is an inevitable reality as Western culture invades Amazonia; the botanical knowledge of Amazonian Indians is disappearing even more rapidly than the plants that compose their extensive pharmacopoeia. The potential of ethnobotanical knowledge for Western medicine is vast, beginning with the development of curare toxins as muscle relaxants that are now used in surgery.

Some efforts are being made to preserve the botanical and medicinal expertise of indigenous peoples. One such project organized by Brij Kothari of Cornell University resulted in a book translated into Quichua and Spanish that could serve as a written record of medicinal plants of northern Ecuador. The subsistence-level farmers and laborers of the Ecuadorian parish of La Esperanza still depend on traditional healers and native medicinal plants, despite a local government health center. The oral tradition of knowledge was disap-

pearing as children spent more time away from home attending
regional rural schools. In 1993 participants in this local project began
gathering information about medicinal plants of the region: vernacular names, local habitats, descriptions, medicinal uses, and methods
for their preparation and administration. The goal was to preserve
botanical knowledge for local use, although during the interviews
some local people noted that certain medicinal plants were becoming difficult to find in local habitats. The book includes drawings of
each plant and symbolic illustrations of its use as an aid to understanding; several hundred copies of the book were published and
distributed to the local communities that contributed information to
serve as a written record of significant medical information.

Maintaining populations of medicinal plants is another way to
preserve local interest and knowledge. Francisco Montes, a Peruvian
ethnobotanist, founded the Sachamama Ethnobotanical Garden outside Iquitos, Peru. The garden provides a sanctuary for more than
one thousand cultivated medicinal plants, and ancient varieties of
medicinal plants are propagated for their long-term survival. Besides
the important work of conserving and cultivating medicinal plants,
some programs at the garden are spiritual in nature. Healing rituals
and mythology provide the backdrop for the development of medicinal plant knowledge and cannot be ignored as "unscientific"; the
desire to preserve local customs may provide more motivation to
conserve tropical biodiversity.

An unfortunate outcome of Western awareness of healing rituals
has been the development of a new type of "ecotourism" in Amazonian regions, organized adventures for Americans and Europeans
who want to experience shamanic ritual and the psychoactive effects
of *ayahuasca* firsthand. Imagine a rain forest excursion led by a cos-
tumed "witch doctor" promising to enlighten American travelers
who are willing to pay for the experience. New Age publications
advertise the virtues of a rain forest experience as spiritualism and
hallucination, but important caveats remain. Such adventures are
designed to impress their participants, and ethnobotanical accuracy

and authenticity are routinely ignored. Furthermore, plants produce potentially dangerous molecules that may have long-term effects when they are consumed by the uninitiated. The commercialization and exposure of traditional medicine and local healing customs under the mistaken guise of tourism will only hasten their demise.

Anthropologists estimate that possibly fifty-five uncontacted tribes still live in remote regions of the Amazon, probably the last place on earth where such tribes exist. These groups are remnants of ancient hunter-gatherer civilizations, what is left of the Indian populations that inhabited Brazil before the Portuguese navigator Pedro Cabal reached the coast of South American in 1500. The demise of Indian populations has come through disease, starvation, slavery, and other hardships introduced during the last four hundred years. Medicinal knowledge has also been depleted as tribes have vanished, and the uncontacted tribes that remain deserve respect and consideration to conserve their culture and ethnobotany.

Ownership of Medicinal Plants and Traditional Knowledge

Whether plants are native to a Western prairie or Brazilian rain forest, their habitats lie within political borders and support the biodiversity that is native to that land. Local biodiversity constitutes a nation's "genetic property," and it includes the medicinal plants that have been known and used for generations. Healing practices have evolved based on the local flora, and the traditional knowledge of native plants constitutes the "intellectual property" of indigenous peoples, but here is the dilemma: Western explorers, both scientists and so-called bio-prospectors, have made plant collections for research and development, paying for neither the plant material nor the local ethnobotanical knowledge that lead them to their collections. This circumstance is the basis for accusations of "bio-piracy" and demands for the fair treatment of developing nations regarding rights to local genetic and intellectual property, since local peoples have neither the legal nor political expertise to protect their interests.

The pattern of exploitation established by the first explorers and colonists continues today in undeveloped countries, but awareness is now focused on the problem. In 1992, the Earth Summit held at Rio de Janeiro launched the global Convention on Biodiversity, an agreement that delineates a global agenda for preserving biodiversity that is now signed by 165 countries. The Convention promotes efforts for preserving the knowledge of traditional medical practices and the development of equitable intellectual property rights for indigenous peoples. The Convention agenda acknowledges the medical importance of traditional healing methods and their preservation. Indigenous peoples own their medicinal knowledge from a practical perspective, and in the past they have been willing to share their expertise; now a consensus is growing that developed nations must respect the ownership of genetic and intellectual property from a legal and financial perspective as well.

Herbal enthusiasts in Western countries can obtain "rain forest remedies" first identified by indigenous peoples, and the local villagers and tribes realize no benefit when their plants are marketed. Plants like the Brazilian *muirapurama* (*Ptychopetalum olacoides*) are mass-marketed through the Internet as herbal remedies (in this case as an aphrodisiac, although the local uses are for rheumatism and dyspepsia). The Convention on Biodiversity specifies minimum payments of 3 to 5 percent of the value of the sales, but most countries do not have a mechanism to enforce the provisions of the agreement. As a result, plants and ethnobotanical knowledge have been subject to theft, insofar as institutions and corporations have now started to patent genetically unmodified tropical plants. One such example is turmeric (*Curcuma longa*), a traditional herb long used for wound healing in Ayurvedic medicine that has now been patented in the United States for the same medical use. The International Plant Medicine Corporation patented *Banisteriopsis caapi* (the woody forest vine used in preparing the hallucinogenic beverage *ayahuasca*) as a plant variety, but their action received criticism worldwide. Some such patents have been challenged because compounds or organisms from the wild are generally regarded as unpatentable.

Secondary compounds from uncultivated medicinal plants are part of the evolutionary history of their habitats, a natural resource that in many cases has been known and grown by the local people who are the stewards of native biodiversity. The use of tropical plants in developing new medicines and technologies is welcome and inevitable, but how can this research and development promise the preservation of biodiversity and the fair treatment of indigenous people? There is no enforceable global policy, so it remains the responsibility of corporations and researchers to work out equitable arrangements with countries in which they conduct biological research. Several possible models exist: The National Cancer Institute provides a "letter of collection" that states their intent to share technology and benefits with the countries in which they collect new medicinal plants. Merck has entered into an agreement with the Instituto National de Biodiversidad in Costa Rica, in which the pharmaceutical company has paid for the privilege of screening plants and will also pay royalties for any drugs that are developed as a result of this research. Through an agreement with the Costa Rican government, profits will help to fund conservation efforts that protect native biodiversity. Using this agreement as a model, biologist Thomas Eisner has established the Biotic Exploration fund to assist developing countries with exploration of the biological resources in their countries. Similar biodiversity institutes could work to catalog local organisms, participate with corporations and research organizations in exploration projects, and do the initial chemical screening processes using fresh plant materials.

Medicinal Plants, Legislation, and the Law

Who owns wild plants? Traditional healers and herbalists alike have gathered certain plants with impunity, but medicinal plants have frequently needed intervention to prevent their overcollection and disappearance. During the Middle Ages, frightening tales about collecting the roots of mandrake (*Mandragora officinarum*) were used to intimidate amateur herbalists; according to legend, the mandrake releases a death-dealing shriek when it is uprooted. In some societies, healers own the medicinal plants that they need to practice medicine, and most people do not collect or cultivate certain specialized medicinal species. In Himalayan villages, there are prohibitions against collecting certain plants during religious festivals, and in some countries like the Congo the collection of rare medicinal plants like *Rauvolfia* species can be done only with a permit.

In the United Kingdom, the Wildlife and Countryside Act of 1981 prohibits the uprooting of any plant other than by the landowner or the landowner's agent, while several medicinal plants can only be collected from the French countryside for commercial sale with a permit from the Ministry of the Environment. The gathering of wild plants from the countryside has frequently been viewed as a right of all citizens; indeed this has been the more common philosophy worldwide. In Switzerland legislation provides the right to collect wild medicinal plants from any land, although commercial collection still requires a local permit. Plants have long been regarded as available for the taking from public and private lands, not as theft in the legal sense. The Theft Act of 1968 is a rare piece of legislation that prohibits collection of plant parts in the United Kingdom for commerce or reward.

Of course, plants are collected from the wild for different reasons; some are valued as medicinal herbs, while others are sought for cultivation. Cycads (Cycadaceae), cacti (Cactaceae), and spurges (Euphorbiaceae) have a range of ethnobotanical uses as foods and medicines, but their status as endangered species is the result of poaching by plant collectors who prize them for their growth forms. All native plants constitute our biological legacy, biodiversity that deserves protection regardless of whether the plants have medicinal or other economic significance. When plant populations begin to decrease, protective legislative and legal solutions may be considered, but these exist only in developed nations; most biodiversity occurs around the equator. In the United States, just 4 percent of the land provides habitats for 38 percent of the species that appear on federal lists of threatened and endangered plants. Frequently there are "hot spots" of particularly high biodiversity, such as the rain forests of the Hawaiian Islands, which are now losing many species as aggressive exotic plants compete with the native vegetation.

The Endangered Species Act recognizes a plant species as endangered only when it is close to extinction, with a population that has been reduced to fewer than 120 individual plants. Presently 702 plants are on the list of endangered species. The Hawaiian Islands alone have 263 rare and endangered plants, including several native plants known locally as *hau,* species of *Hibiscus* and *Hibiscadelphus* with uninvestigated ethnobotanical uses. Besides those on the federal list, many other Hawaiian species are on the verge of extinction and will be saved only by bringing them into cultivation in upland nurseries. In most cases, legal protection means that the individual plants and their habitat must be protected; in this way one federally protected endangered species serves as a safety "umbrella" for other native plants and animals in the same ecosystem.

Medicinal plants have been a particular concern because they can disappear from their habitats through overcollection for commercial trade. In a few countries, specific laws protect jeopardized medicinal species, such as *Rauvolfia serpentina* in India, but international trade agreements are particularly useful in helping to stem the trade in species that are now threatened or endangered. The Convention on International Trade in Endangered Species of Wild Fauna and Flora (CITES) now has a membership of 144 countries that seek to avoid the exploitation of plants and animals that are traded internationally. CITES provides a list of plants and animals that are threatened with extinction or otherwise imperiled as a result of trade; their trade is controlled by a licensing system. Trade in certain endangered species and related products is banned, including the oil from the composite *Saussurea lappa* that is popular in Asia and the Middle East as an aphrodisiac and treatment for skin diseases. Trade in the roots of American ginseng (*Panax quinquefolius;* Plate 22) is also regulated by the CITES treaty.

Botanic Gardens, Seed Banks, and Cultivation

For centuries, botany and medicine were essentially the same profession because plants were the major medicinal sources. Physic gardens such as the Giardino dei Semplice (Garden of Simples) at Florence provided the plants and drugs necessary for medical instruction, and the first botanic gardens were the living collections of medicinal plants cultivated at universities in western Europe during the sixteenth century. Even in nineteenth-century America, medical students still attended lectures in botany, a practical science for physicians who would have to know and use botanical compounds.

From their earliest beginnings as living collections, botanic gardens are again important as places to cultivate and preserve rare or endangered medicinal species. Plant populations worldwide are being depleted through collection and habitat loss. Medicinal plants are even disappearing from the sacred groves of Asia, ancient forest preserves that are protected habitats for many plants needed in traditional medicine. When wild populations disappear, genetic variation is lost, and extinction of the species is a greater likelihood, but garden cultivation can postpone extinction for many plant species in the same way that zoos can protect endangered animals. Clearly this option is a last resort, but for many medicinal plants cultivation and seed-saving may be the only pathway to their long-term survival. New gardens will be needed to protect more of the tropical endangered plants because although most endangered plants occur in equatorial countries, there are relatively few tropical botanic gardens in South America and Africa; only about 230 botanic gardens of 1400 gardens worldwide occur in the tropics.

Some gardens are exclusively devoted to plants with ethnobotanical or medical uses. The Amy B. H. Greenwell Ethnobotanical Garden of the Bishop Museum in Hawaii includes 250 plants used by Hawaiians, both native Hawaiian and introduced Polynesian species, including several that appear on the federal list of endangered plants. About 1600 medicinal plant species are cultivated at the Tokyo Metropolitan Medicinal Plants Garden, and the Tropical Botanic Garden and Research Institute in Trivandrum, India, has worked to propagate 650 rare medicinal plant species that can be distributed to institutions and growers for cultivation. Medicinal gardens are common in Russia, Poland, and other countries of eastern Europe in which the practice of herbal medicine remains strong. Traditional healing in China also depends extensively on medicinal plants, and there are several Chinese medicinal gardens such as the one at the Institute for Medicinal Plant Development in Beijing.

Besides providing habitats for growing plants, botanic gardens can serve as gene banks in which seeds can be maintained and stored for eventual cultivation or research in selection and breeding. Seeds can be stored under controlled conditions and still retain their viability, possibly for hundreds of years. The seed bank at Gatersleben in Germany includes more than 2000 cultivated and wild medicinal plants, but most seed banks do not have particular collections of medicinal plants that have been selected for preservation. As seed bank collections are being gathered for long-term storage, plants used in traditional medicine should receive particular priority.

Eventually all widely used medicinal plants will need to be cultivated to supply the growing demand in developed nations for plant-derived medicines. Cultivation will help to preserve the remaining wild populations of medicinal plants, and there are medicinal benefits as well. Medicinal plants can be grown under uniform plantation conditions, harvested at the correct time, and dried efficiently to preserve their chemistry; cultivars of medicinal plants can be developed for particular chemical concentrations and properties. As with all plants of economic importance, the genetic diversity held by wild populations may eventually be needed for developing new medicinal varieties or disease-resistant strains. Whether temperate or tropical, wild populations can be depleted quickly when a species is in high demand, a pattern that has been repeated several times in the history of medicinal botany. Following the discoveries of feverbark (*Cinchona* spp.), tropical yams (*Dioscorea* spp.), and snakeroot (*Rauvolfia serpentina*), wild populations disappeared from their habitats; cultivation is the only way to prevent the loss of known medicinal plants as a result of overcollection.

An alternative to plant cultivation in the strict sense is tissue culture. This technique is another form of "cultivation," in which the cells of medicinal plants are laboratory-propagated under sterile conditions, far from the soil and spades of a field or physic garden. Growth conditions of tissue cultures can be controlled to produce maximum concentrations of medicinal secondary compounds, and this technology may prove to be the most efficient way to produce the quantities of specific botanical compounds that will be needed in the future.

Medicinal plants are part of the earth's biodiversity, remarkable organisms that evolved secondary compounds as defense mechanisms that allowed them to survive in nature. The secondary compounds that cause them to be valued as medicinal sources also leave them vulnerable to destruction. The selfsame molecules are the basis of plant survival in natural ecosystems, the demand for plants as medicines, and now the need for medicinal plant conservation and cultivation. Human medicinal needs and desires are important, but the conservation of botanical biodiversity should guide our actions; we cannot replace these species when they vanish. Medicinal plants with the potential to improve and save lives deserve our particular attention and protection.

CHAPTER 10

~~~~~~

Herbal Histories, Considerations, and Caveats

T HE GARDEN tomato (*Lycopersicon esculentum*) was once an esteemed medicinal herb with an interesting early history. During the first half of the nineteenth century, tomatoes were introduced from the highlands of northern Chile, Peru, and Ecuador. At first they did not appeal to New England palates, and early growers often fed the fruit to their pigs. In 1835, tomato fortunes reversed when Dr. John Cook Bennett described them as "the most healthy article of the Materia Alimentary" useful in treating dyspepsia, cholera, and bilious attacks. He predicted that soon the active principles would be available in pill form, and by 1837 Dr. Archibald Miles of Cincinnati marketed a Compound Extract of Tomato, advertised as containing "hepatine" that stimulated "the organs of secretion and excretion." Competition soon appeared as Dr. Phelps Compound Tomato Pills, which promised to cure everything from "gravel" (kidney stones), colic, and influenza to fevers, nervous diseases, and acid stomach. Drs. Miles and Phelps accused each other of selling adulterated products, and there were even mutual claims that certain tomato pills contained no tomatoes! The battles soon subsided, but not until tomatoes were well publicized as healthy vegetables to grow and consume. Bostonians purchased more than a half ton of tomato seeds in 1851, and soon tomatoes made a successful transition from unproven medicinal herb to popular table food.

Not every herbal remedy boasts outlandish medicinal claims (nor do all medicinal herbs have the potential to become standard salad ingredients), but there are lessons to be learned from the popularity, publicity, notoriety, and mid-nineteenth century *denouement* of tomato pills. The promises made by purveyors of tomato pills were typical of the nineteenth century, an era of patent medicines and unproven remedies with exaggerated, even bogus, claims. Since the time of the earliest humans, cultures have relied on plants to supply medicines, so it is no surprise that the tomato became an object of herbal attention. It was a fruit new to North America, brightly colored, and worthy of interest; it fit anthropologists' profile of a "salient plant," a species that attracts attention. The vines are hairy, pungent, and bitter to taste. They produce high concentrations of secondary compounds, which are there for the tasting and experimenting. These typical physical characteristics seem to direct human attention to a plant as a possible medicinal source, according to cultural anthropologists.

It is not a coincidence that medicinal herbs are frequently aromatic, with a distinctive taste, texture, growth form, or other marked trait, such a tendency to cause dermatitis. As salient plants, they are "obvious" in the wild and frequently attract more interaction and use than other species. Indigenous people do not seem to

Figure 10-1. Tomatoes (*Lycopersicon esculentum*) were viewed with suspicion as a food during the first half of the nineteenth century, but they soon became the primary ingredient in popular herbal pills marketed with exaggerated medical claims.

select plants for medicinal use randomly; in fact, many plants without salient features are simply ignored. In short, the selection of plants to sample for medicinal use is the result of the secondary compounds that plants produce. Often these chemicals are packaged in surface hairs, which release pungent compounds when they are crushed. This selection process is reminiscent of the way that many insects and animals choose plants for consumption or egg-laying, based on plant chemistry rather than visual cues.

How different were nineteenth-century tomato pills from herbal medicines marketed now? We might be amused at the idea of tomatoes as a Victorian panacea, but the claims of some current remedies are not far afield. A brief perusal of modern advertising and literature on alternative medicine yields some dubious examples, from "fossilized plant" minerals to "sacred" plants and herbal products with all manner of implied medicinal claims. What we need to remember is this: Medicine is a branch of science, and medicinal plants and their compounds are within the scientific realms of botany and chemistry. Medicinal herbs have nothing inherently magical in them, whether they were first used by shamans, Native Americans, or Europeans. They are ordinary plants that survive in nature because they have evolved secondary compounds which protect them from predators and competitors; some of those compounds are nontoxic enough for us to use as medicines, and these are the basis of medicinal botany.

For centuries, herbalism has been fraught with notions of magic, legend, and innuendo, a conundrum of natural chemistry and culture. In fact, herbalism is part of the biological continuum of botanical defense mechanisms and medicinal botany. The aroma of an herbal tea mixture has the same ecological explanation as the ginkgolide compounds in *Ginkgo* capsules, the morphine in opium, or the toxins in a poisonous hemlock; they are all secondary compounds with specific evolutionary functions. Their medicinal uses are merely fortunate ramifications of their natural history.

Essential Herbs

The history of herbalism is the history of medicine, since plants were the *materia medica* available to the first physicians. Often these early cures worked well, and the same plants are being used today for similar medical applications. The common roadside yarrow (*Achillea millefolium;* Plate 1) illustrates the medicinal breadth of an ancient herb: According to legend, the Homeric hero Achilles used yarrow to staunch the flow of blood from battle wounds, and the genus *Achillea* commemorates his name. We now know that *Achillea* has anti-inflammatory and hemostatic properties, and it is a genus that has been used medicinally by indigenous cultures worldwide. In Europe, yarrow was brewed into an herbal tea for internal bleeding, fevers, and indigestion, and the Micmac Indians drank yarrow with warm milk to cure colds. More than one hundred biologically active secondary compounds have been isolated from yarrows, including some toxic compounds like thujone, but moderate doses of yarrow tea apparently are not dangerous.

Yarrow was among the herbs that substituted for pharmaceutical drugs in England during World War II. Because many European countries were occupied and supply shipments were curtailed, England experienced shortages of critical pharmaceutical drugs during the early 1940s. Staff at the Royal Botanic Gardens, Kew, responded by organizing a national scheme for collecting medicinal plants from the rural areas of England. The National Federation of Women's Institutes and the Boy Scouts provided information on plant identification and assisted with the early collection efforts. In 1941 the Ministry of Health appointed a Vegetable Drugs Committee "to review the present and future of vegetable drugs in the light of Empire consumption . . . to consider the steps which should be taken to secure organization and collection, and to make recommendations to the Minister." The Committee developed lists by county of native and naturalized medicinal plants and recruited more groups such as the Scottish Women's Rural Institutes, schoolchildren, scouts, and guides that were able to scour the countryside to collect the listed plants. The Vegetable Drugs Committee provided detailed instructions on herb drying and storage, since secondary compounds can deteriorate quickly if the plant material is not handled correctly after collection.

During the war years, British plants were used to treat ailments ranging from tapeworm, constipation, and gout to heart disease, wounds, and nervous complaints. Sought-after plants included some highly toxic species that are medicinal when administered in con-trolled doses: foxglove (*Digitalis purpurea*), aconite (*Aconitum lapellus*), black henbane (*Hyoscyamus niger*), and thorn apple or Jimson weed (*Datura stramonium*). More benign herbs included valerian (*Valeriana officinalis;* Plate 28), wild thyme (*Thymus polytrichus*), burdock (*Arctium* spp.), and black horehound (*Ballota nigra*). Drying was an important part of the collection work. Foxglove in particular requires rapid drying to preserve its cardiac glycosides from breakdown; a pam-phlet from Kew advised temperatures between 90° and 100°F with the fresh plants arranged on wooden frames covered with wire netting or lace curtains. Laundry rooms, sheds, and outhouses were outfitted with coke-burning stoves for efficient drying once the various plants were gath-ered from fields and hedge-rows. County herb committees organized local collections with the supervision of the

Figure 10-2. During World War II, black henbane (*Hyoscyamus niger*) was among the species that the Vegetable Drugs Committee iden-tified as a medicinal plant worthy of collection from rural areas of England.

Ministry of Health, and the Ministry of Supply issued a monthly *Herb Collectors Bulletin*. The *Bulletin* provided details about which plants to gather and prepare for shipment, progress of plant collections in the various rural counties, and methods for conserving medical supplies. The first *Bulletin* (1942) noted that in Derbyshire "the Hathersage Women's Institutes dried fifty pounds of material chiefly nettles in the attic of a house, and the Clifton and Mayfield Boy Scouts dried seventy-six pounds of foxglove leaves at their headquarters. They hope to do much more this year and the county committee is looking around for collecting depots." With the help of willing civilians who learned field botany, wild medicinal herbs supplied England for the duration of the war.

Long before World War II, settlers from Europe arriving in the New World carried with them herbs that they would need and quickly learned the plants of their new land. Martha Ballard, a midwife in Maine during the late eighteenth and early nineteenth centuries, recorded several healing plants in her diary. These herbs helped mothers and infants survive the rigors of labor and birth and the subsequent risk of infection, and several of them were probably effective medicinal plants. *A Midwife's Tale* (1990) by Laura Thatcher Ulrich describes Ballard's work; in her practice she used wild or cultivated medicinal herbs such as dock (*Rumex* spp.), mullein (*Verbascum thapsus*), plantain (*Plantago* spp.), wormwood (*Artemisia annua*), sumac (*Rhus* spp.), basswood (*Tilia americana*), and burdock (*Arctium* spp.), and she purchased botanical drugs such as camphor (*Cinnamomum camphora*) and aloe (*Aloe* spp.). Burdock is a diuretic and its seeds may have antibiotic properties, basswood is valued for its soothing properties, and wormwood was known historically as a stimulant in tonics. Ballard gathered these herbs as a midwife, and more than one hundred years later the same plants or their close relatives were collected by the wartime county herb committees during a national medical crisis in England.

During the nineteenth century, there were alternatives to herbal medicines that were dangerous and ineffective. Dr. Benjamin Rush, an esteemed physician and signer of the Declaration of Independence, advocated the use of calomel; these ubiquitous pills contained mercurous chloride that left patients with the devastating symptoms of mercury poisoning. Various alternative treatments evolved during the nineteenth century, as a result of medical misconceptions and the prevailing distrust of bad practices such as the use of calomel. Dr. Samuel Thomson, a New Hampshire farmer and physician, developed the "Thomsonian system" of therapy in which he advocated purging, steam baths, and use of Indian tobacco (*Lobelia inflata*) as an emetic. He advocated healing without the "pernicious and fatal effects of the mineral poisons," referring to the toxic effects of calomel, but he was essentially a charlatan whose marketing techniques provided opportunities for other purveyors of herbal medicines.

Lydia Pinkham of Lynn, Massachusetts, marketed her Vegetable Compound for women experiencing reproductive problems and exhaustion. Her preparation was a patent medicine of macerated herbs in 19 percent alcohol, and there may have been some validity to her claims. The original ingredients included unicorn root or star grass (*Aletris farinosa*) and black cohosh (*Cimicifuga racemosa;* Plate 13), which seem to promote the activity of female reproductive hormones. Like tropical yams used in the first oral contraceptives, the genus *Aletris* contains the steroid diosgenin, which resembles the chemical structure of estrogen. Two other ingredients, however, were potentially dangerous; golden ragwort (*Senecio aureus*) synthesizes toxic pyrrolizidine alkaloids, and butterfly weed (*Asclepias tuberosa;* Plate 8) produces cardiac glycosides. It is unclear what a toxic dose might have been, but Lydia E. Pinkham's Vegetable Compound was sold successfully from 1875 through the 1960s. Using testimonial advertising, women who had suffered from "sick headache," "nervous breakdown," "womb trouble," and other reproductive complaints were featured in Vegetable Compound advertisements. Engravings of Pinkham appeared in newspaper advertisements and pharmacy displays, and she was memorialized during the 1880s by the Dartmouth glee club refrain, "Oh, we'll sing of Lydia Pinkham, /

And her love for the human race, / How she sells her Vegetable Compound, / And the papers they publish her face."

Doses and Efficacy

Two questions have confounded us since the first human sampled a medicinal plant: Do herbal remedies work? How much should a patient ingest for an effective, safe cure? Americans spend millions of dollars each year on herbal products that are marketed as food supplements, but in most cases, consumers do not really know chemically what they are purchasing or using. Selecting from the capsules, extracts, and teas in a health food store is not unlike facing a forest of unknown medicinal species; no one can vouch for efficacy, and the "active ingredients" may vary from batch to batch with the chemical variations among the plants in the herbal products.

In the United States the Dietary Supplement Health and Education Act of 1994 allows purveyors to sell herbs and plant extracts without the prior approval of the Food and Drug Administration, and since then the market for herbal supplements has been meteoric in its growth. This rapid growth might be in part attributable to increased interest in treatments that are alternatives to mainstream medicine. In the present compromise, the Food and Drug Administration takes products off the market only after they have proven to be toxic, and companies that sell herbs will not make unsubstantiated specific claims about the medical benefits of a particular herbal product. Regardless, many such products do bear implied medical claims on their packaging (or such claims are proffered in pamphlets or Internet sites provided by the same company). Under the 1994 act, general claims are permissible; saw palmetto (*Serenoa serrulata*) labels may claim "prostate health," but cannot imply a cure for prostate cancer. Feverfew (*Tanacetum parthenium*) capsules may help with "brain function," but not "cure migraines." There is also complete freedom in naming herbal products. Obviously these are areas open to interpretation, but marketing for herbal products often errs on the side of overstatement.

There is a clear recommendation for *caveat emptor* when purchasing herbal products in the United States. Some purveyors have based their herbal supplements on anecdotal reports or unproven ethnobotanical evidence, rather than on years of dependable use or controlled studies that demonstrate efficacy. Unproven remedies are common in the marketplace, and skepticism is warranted until research proves the accuracy of various medical claims. Articles tout *dong quai* (*Angelica polymorpha*) and chaste tree (*Vitex agnus-castus*) for female reproductive problems, passion flower (*Passiflora incarnata*) for anxiety and high blood pressure, and cat's claw (*Uncaria tomentosa*) for arthritis, asthma, and cancer. The chemistry and efficacy of these plants are relatively unknown, and there is the chance of toxicity or overdose until the secondary compounds are known and understood.

The matter of dose is particularly perplexing. A recent analysis of ginseng products revealed a ten-fold variation in the concentration of biologically active molecules, although the products were labeled as containing identical amounts. Standard doses are neither defined nor regulated by the Food and Drug Administration, and there can be disagreement about which chemical constituents of a medicinal herb should be standardized. Some companies have relied on research from Germany, where there has been considerable interest in isolating and understanding the mode of action of the individual compounds in herbs. Both physicians and patients should know what active ingredients are in herbal supplements. How else can dose be prescribed or regulated?

In Germany, 70 percent of physicians prescribe herbal remedies for their patients, but in Germany and France, herbal medicines are subject to licensing, and there are clearly fewer "unknowns" when herbs are used to treat a particular ailment. German government involvement has resulted in thorough research and consistent gathering of information; the German Health Authorities, the equivalent of our Food and Drug Administration, has established a panel known as Commission E to oversee herbal medicines in Germany. The American Botanical Council published the first English translation of the German Commission E monographs, a review of 324 medicinal herbs that includes information on efficacy, side effects, precautions, contraindications, medical interactions, and dose. The conclusion is obvious: In European countries, regulation and licensing have led to greater and more effective use of these important medicinal plants. Physicians use herbs along with pharmaceutical drugs, and in Europe these two medical realms converge into one pharmacopoeia. In reality, many herbs are used medicinally and not as food supplements; it is reasonable that these herbs should be treated as drugs considering their chemistry and potential effects. In the United States, we have the same opportunity to regulate herbal claims, chemical constituents, and purity, which would lead to the more effective and comprehensive use of herbs to treat human disease. There has been no difficulty in gaining acceptance for botanical drugs such as reserpine, curare, morphine, and paclitaxel, once their chemistry and mode of action are known. Before most U.S. physicians will prescribe herbal remedies for their patients, specific medical information and chemically standardized products must be available. This information would clear the muddy waters of unsubstantiated claims, unknown chemistry, unregulated doses, and unpredictable risks and open new possibilities for the use of herbs in Western medicine.

Plant Toxins and Risks

Botanical secondary compounds are not benign molecules; ecologically speaking, these evolved as chemical defenses that can repel, sicken, stun, poison, stunt, maim, or kill other species. We are naive to think of every plant extract as necessarily safe for human ingestion, and poison centers know firsthand numerous examples of botanical toxins. Amateur herb collectors have unknowingly gathered the leaves of false hellebore (*Veratrum viride*) or water hemlock (*Cicuta maculata*) for "spring tonics" with lethal results. Even though both these plants have been used medicinally, they can be lethal in uncontrolled doses. As we discussed in earlier chapters, dose is often the factor that distinguishes an effective medicine from a deadly poison. Dose itself, however, is often a vague concept when dealing with herbal medicines. A recent article on women's health recommended using homemade teas of poison hemlock (*Conium maculatum*) for breast tenderness and *nux vomica* (*Strychnos nux-vomica*, the source of strychnine) for morning sickness. Perhaps a small quantity of weak tea will do no harm, but what happens to the patient who drinks several brimming cups of well-steeped poison brew?

No doubt consumers of herbal medicines sometimes have been sold toxins and misinformation. Even some plants with a long history of use have been implicated as potentially toxic; sassafras (*Sassafras albidum*) contains safrole, a carcinogen that has now been banned by the Food and Drug Administration, and high doses of comfrey (*Symphytum officinale;* Plate 26) can cause liver damage. Two other medicinal herbs that may cause acute liver damage are creosote bush (*Larrea divaricata*), long used to brew chaparral tea, and germander (*Teucrium canadense*), an ingredient in herbal mixtures used by dieters. Yohimbe (*Corynanthe yohimbe*) is used as a dietary supplement and aphrodisiac, but it is suspected of causing seizures, kidney failure, and death. The alkaloid ephedrine in species of *Ephedra* (often marketed as *ma huang*) increases heart rate and blood pressure

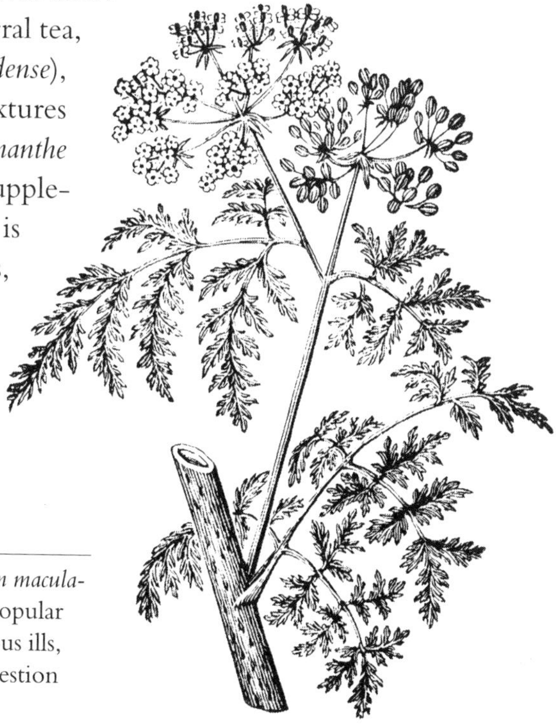

Figure 10-3. Poison hemlock (*Conium maculatum*) has been recommended in the popular herbal literature as a remedy for various ills, but it contains toxic alkaloids and ingestion can be lethal.

and has proven fatal when high amounts have been ingested. *Ephedra* has long been used to brew effective teas for colds and hayfever, but its prolonged use in herbal extracts or mixtures promising weight loss or more energy may prove hazardous. Even more dangerous are the recreational *Ephedra* products that promise psychological effects. The latter have been implicated in several deaths, and as a result, the Food and Drug Administration has sought strict regulation of *Ephedra*-containing products.

The berries of pokeweed (*Phytolacca americana*) were once used to make a tea for arthritis and dysentery, and its roots were poulticed for skins ailments and bruises and used as an emetic. Pokeweed is now known to contain phytolaccatoxin, which affects cell division and may cause chromosome damage and severe blood aberrations. The shoots were a common spring potherb in the South, and children still crush poke berries to release their deep pink juice. Cooking breaks down the toxin, but it is present in the fresh leaves, stems, and roots; phytochemists now advise against skin contact with any part of this dangerous plant. The list of medicinal plants that can cause damage in the name of healing is impressive. Of course, toxic effects are frequently the result of high dose, but individual physiology and the concentrations of active chemicals may vary, leading to potential health hazards.

Another potential problem is contamination, either by accident or intent, in medicinal plant collections. Foxglove (*Digitalis purpurea*) has shown up as an adulterant in herbal mixtures where it is not among the listed ingredients, and Asian herbal remedies tainted with heavy metals have been found for sale in the United States. When herbs are imported from China or through Hong Kong herb dealers, substitutions of one species for another may occur in the process. No standardized system of nomenclature for herbs exists, and visual inspection of the dried plant material does not always reveal adulteration or misidentification of the dried plant material. In "Alternative Medicine—The Risks of Untested and Unregulated Remedies," an editorial in *The New England Journal of Medicine* (17 September 1998),

Marcia Angell and Jerome Kassirer noted the case of a diabetic who developed lead poisoning from an Indian herbal remedy for diabetes. They argue for rigorous medical trials, scrupulous labeling, and monitoring for safety and efficacy of herbal remedies. Citing the lack of information about marketed herbal medicines, they comment, "Now, with the increased interest in alternative medicine, we see a reversion to irrational approaches to medical practice, even while scientific medicine is making some of its most dramatic advances." As emigrants from countries like Mexico, China, and Cambodia arrive in the United States, the herbal practices associated with traditional healing are also transplanted. Small shops sell various imported herbal remedies, and urban physicians are discovering that their patients sometimes augment their medical treatment with the services of a folk healer. Part of this may be a placebo effect; we really do not know the effectiveness of the botanical medicines that are being sold. In other instances some physicians acknowledge that folk healers can help sick patients, by allaying fears and treating psychological and even physical symptoms.

A Summation

Are we reverting to a medical Middle Ages? Certainly there is now an overwhelming interest in healing herbs, in part the result of a growing distrust of mainstream Western medicine. Some firmly believe that traditional healers know more than oncologists and cardiologists and that shamanic huts surpass hospital wards. There is also a sense that government is holding back valuable therapies as part of a bureaucratic reluctance to share new medical options, but it was that same concern in the Food and Drug Administration that kept thalidomide out of the United States during the 1960s and prevented many devastating birth defects. New medicinal chemicals should be viewed with anticipation of their benefits and with suspicion of their potential dangers, and the definition of a medicinal chemical should include the secondary compounds of plants.

Figure 10-4. A woodcut from the title page of *The Grete Herball* (1526) illustrated "male" and "female" anthropomorphic mandrakes based on characteristics of the taproots, although Peter Treveris cautioned his readers against medicinal "fraude."

The contemporary approach to alternative medicine resembles attitudes toward many therapies touted during the nineteenth century when medical quacks advocated all sorts of therapies, from Thomsonian emetics to animal magnetism. A trusting nineteenth-century public served as willing medical subjects, but often with disappointing results. Now we have the tools to gather information and evaluate the effectiveness of medicines; why not use research laboratories to understand the chemistry and mode of action of medical compounds, including those from medicinal plants? Our motivation should be a view of the future, the outcome of the possible synergy between traditional medicine and modern research. It does seem regressive to use medicines for which the neither efficacy, mode of action, nor effective dose are known. We can learn from the expertise of traditional healers and indigenous peoples; their knowledge will combine with Western medical tradition to yield a global understanding of medicinal plants, their uses, and the chemistry of medicinal compounds.

Plants are remarkable organisms. Their natural history includes subtle biological warfare with their competitors, and secondary compounds are the by-product of these struggles. These diverse molecules cycle in nature and define many groups of plants that have evolved on earth. As a splendid coincidence, we can draw upon the chemical diversity of botanical molecules to supply ourselves with effective medicines.

Glossary

Abortifacient. Anything used to terminate a pregnancy prematurely

Adaptogenic. Allows the human body to adapt to stressful conditions

Analgesic. Provides pain relief

Antibiotic. Kills or halts the growth of microorganisms

Antiseptic. Prevents putrefaction or decay, stops the growth of microorganisms

Astringent. Causes tissues to contract

Bioactive. Has an effect upon a living organism

Cardiotonic. Controls heart beat and the contraction of heart muscle

Contraceptive. Anything used to prevent pregnancy

Decoction. A liquid preparation made by boiling leaves, roots, or other plant parts in water

Diuretic. Increases the production of urine

Emetic. Induces vomiting

Hemostatic. Stops the flow of blood

Infusion. A tea made by soaking leaves, roots, or other plant parts in cold or hot water

Pathogen. A microorganism that causes disease

Psychotropic. Has an altering effect on the mind

Purgative. Works as a cathartic or laxative

Soporific. Causes sleep

Vasodilation. Causes blood vessels to dilate rather than constrict

Further Reading

Akerle, Olayiwola, Vernon Heywood, and Hugh Synge, eds. *The Conservation of Medicinal Plants: Proceedings of an International Consultation 21–27 March Held at Chiang Mai, Thailand.* Cambridge: Cambridge University Press, 1991.

Arber, Agnes. *Herbals: Their Origin and Evolution, A Chapter in the History of Botany 1470–1670* (Cambridge Science Classics). Cambridge: Cambridge University Press, 1987 (reissue of the 1938 revised edition of the classic text published in 1912).

Arvigo, Rosita, and Michael J. Balick. *Rain-Forest Remedies, One Hundred Healing Herbs of Belize,* ed. 2. Twin Lakes, Wisconsin: Lotus Press, 1998.

Balick, Michael J., Elaine Elisabetsky, and Sarah A. Laird, eds. *Medicinal Resources of the Tropical Forest: Biodiversity and Its Importance to Human Health.* New York: Columbia University Press, 1995.

Berenbaum, May R. *Bugs in the System.* Reading, Massachusetts: Addison-Wesley, 1995.

Blumenthal, Mark, and Robert Rister, eds. *The Complete German Commission E Monographs: Therapeutic Monographs on Medicinal Plants for Human Use.* Austin, Texas: American Botanical Council, 1997.

Blunt, Wilfred, and Sandra Raphael. *The Illustrated Herbal.* London: Thames and Hudson, 1979.

Budavari, Susan, ed. *The Merck Index, An Encyclopedia of Chemicals, Drugs, and Biologicals,* 12th ed. Whitehouse Station, New Jersey: Merck Research Laboratories, 1996.

Erichsen-Brown, Charlotte. *Medicinal and Other Uses of North American Plants.* New York: Dover, 1979.

Etkin, Nina. *Eating on the Wild Side: The Pharmacologic, Ecologic, and Social Implications of Using Noncultigens,* Tucson: University of Arizona, 1994.

Foster, Steven, and James A. Duke. *A Field Guide to Medicinal Plants, Eastern and Central North America,* Boston: Houghton Mifflin, 1990.

Fowler, Gene, ed. *Mystic Healers and Medicine Shows, Blazing Trails to Wellness in the Old West and Beyond,* Santa Fe: Ancient City Press, 1997.

Gruenwald, George, Thomas Brendler, and Christof Jaenicke, eds. *PDR for Herbal Medicines.* Montvale, New Jersey: Medical Economics Company, 1998.

Joyce, Christopher. *Earthly Goods, Medicine-Hunting in the Rainforest.* Boston: Little, Brown, 1994.

Lewis, Walter H., and Memory P. F. Elvin-Lewis. *Medical Botany, Plants Affecting Man's Health.* New York: John Wiley and Sons, 1977.

Martin, Gary. *Ethnobotany and Plant Conservation, A Methods Manual.* New York: Chapman and Hall, 1994.

Miller, Amy Bess. *Shaker Medicinal Herbs, A Compendium of History, Lore, and Uses.* Pownal, Vermont: Storey Books, 1998.

Millspaugh, Charles F. *American Medicinal Plants.* New York: Dover, 1974 (reissue of the original 1892 two-volume work *Medicinal Plants,* published by John C. Yorston and Company, Philadelphia).

Moerman, Daniel. *Native American Ethnobotany.* Portland, Oregon: Timber Press, 1998.

Morton, Julia F. *Major Medicinal Plants: Botany, Culture, and Uses.* Springfield, Illinois: Charles C. Thomas, 1977.

Nigg, Herbert N., and David Seigler, eds. *Phytochemical Resources for Medicine and Agriculture.* New York: Plenum Press, 1992.

Plotkin, Mark. *Tales of a Shaman's Apprentice.* New York: Viking, 1993.

Schultes, Richard Evans, and Robert F. Raffauf. *The Healing Forest,* Portland, Oregon: Dioscorides Press, 1990.

Schultes, Richard Evans, and Siri von Reis, eds. *Ethnobotany, Evolution of a Discipline.* Portland, Oregon: Dioscorides Press, 1995.

Usher, George. 1974. *Dictionary of Plants Used by Man.* New York: Hafner Press, 1974.

Whistler, W. Arthur. *Polynesian Herbal Medicine.* Lawai, Hawaii: National Tropical Botanical Garden, 1992.

Index